CAIRO PAPERS IN SOCIAL SCIENCE

Volume 29, Number I, Spring 2006

Crossing Borders, Shifting Boundaries

Palestinian Dilemmas

Edited by

Sari Hanafi

Contributions by
Sheerin al-Araj
Mohamed Kamel Doraï
Cédric Parizot
Tamara Tamimi
Mary Totry

The American University in Cairo Press
Cairo   New York

Cover map: Ola Seif

Dar el Kutub No. 27291/07
ISBN 978-977-416-184-1

Printed in Egypt

Contents

Acknowledgments

The AUTHORS express their gratitude to the Palestinian Diaspora and Refugee Center, Shaml (Ramallah) and to the International Development Research Center (IDRC) (Ottawa-Canada) for their valuable support for the project of this book. Special thanks to all of those who provided their advice and suggestions, and spent time discussing the ideas in this manuscript, especially Riina Isotalo, Rula El-Rifai, Pamela Scholey, Salim Tamari and Mick Dumper.

Sites mentioned in the text

Chapter 1
Introduction
Return Migration and the Burden of Borders

Sari Hanafi

THE PAPERS in this collection are mainly the outcome of a project carried out by the Palestinian Diaspora and Refugee Center (Shaml) under my direction and continued later on when I was at the American University of Beirut. The project was sponsored by International Development Research Center (IDRC, Ottawa, Canada),[1] and centered on the effort to understand the issue of return migration to Palestine from a sociological point of view.

The papers grouped here are part of the background to that project in that they examine various human situations among Palestinians, ranging from inhabitants villages that have been divided by borders such as the "Green Line" (the 1949 armistice line) to populations of Palestinian origin that have been cut off from their roots in Palestine and are now seeking to establish their lives and those of their children outside Palestine and even outside the Arab world. The final two papers deal with real and virtual efforts at return to Palestine by two quite different groups (youth and professional experts). The theme that runs through these papers is thus the role of borders and boundaries—those that people seek to cross and those that

---

1   I am very grateful to Shaml and to the IDRC for making this project possible. Special thanks to all of those who provided their advice and suggestions, especially Nicholas Hopkins, Daoud Barakat, Rula El-Rifai, Iman Hamdy, Riina Isotalo, Cédric Parizot, Pamela Scholey and finally my wife Manal Kortam. The contributions of the authors reflect only their views.

the wider political processes establish around existing populations (such as the Green Line and the new line represented by the Israeli wall). On the one hand, people are moving and, on the other, they are developing survival strategies to deal with new political "shadow lines"[2] that impede their movement. Freedom of movement and its lack are part of the sociological base whose knowledge is necessary for the understanding of choices regarding return migration, i.e., migration back to geographic Palestine if not back to the original home situation.

The papers are also contributions to the dilemmas that faced different segments of the Palestinian population in the period preceding the construction of the Israeli wall beginning in 2005, which further cut up and divided the Palestinian areas and prevented some of the patterns of movement that had emerged since the Oslo agreement (the "Declaration of Principles") in 1993. Since the Palestinian situation is in constant flux, this historical moment has to be kept in mind while reading these papers.

Palestinian Refugees: Movement and Return

The return of refugees to their country of origin seen as a "natural" and thus "problem free" process is one of the major misleading myths surrounding the process of repatriation in the imaginaries of many refugees and Palestinian politicians, and of course not only in the Palestinian case but elsewhere. This collection addresses this issue by placing it in the broader context of movement across or around borders by Palestinians. The broader conclusion is that networks and relationships with other people as social capital are as important as a nostalgic sense of place in understanding voluntary migration, forced migration, and return migration.

By drawing insights from various disciplinary approaches to borders, boundaries, and social networks, this volume sets out to analyze the manifold implications of some socio-economic and cultural factors for an eventual Palestinian return migration. Boundaries are symbolic, cultural, and social, constituting a cognitive or mental geography which influences the transnational ties between different Palestinian communities and shapes their identities. By the same token, the impermeability of some borders has constructed and reinvented new boundaries of difference and distinctiveness among these communities. First, displacement and separation of refugees from the place

---

2 Amitav Ghosh's novel describes Bengal as having been divided between India and Pakistan in 1947 by arbitrarily drawn boundaries, which he calls "shadow lines" because they do not correspond to any social difference (Ghosh 1988).

of origin inevitably created new boundaries between them and those who remained. Second, the institutions and readjustments of geopolitical borders after 1948 and 1967 foster the emergence of such boundaries. Finally, the crossing of borders separating refugees from their place of origin entails power relations and conflicts that reinforce boundaries between groups. Some boundaries remain, some are invented, some are remembered: this is the burden of borders in this highly partitioned part of the world.

This issue of *Cairo Papers in Social Science* includes contributions of scholars who have addressed directly or indirectly the question of the movement of the Palestinian populations over the sixty-year period since the first exodus in 1948 and the different identities they have developed. There have been several waves of refugees caused by the expanding power of Israel, migrations of Palestinian men and sometimes families in search of better economic circumstances in the Arab world and beyond, and movements of individuals across borders to profit from the differences between the two sides of a border. With all this, there is a yearning to return to the point of departure.

While some Palestinians have been able to return to Palestine under the auspices of the Palestinian National Authority or otherwise, others have found their movements restricted by shifts in the internal map of Palestine, and still others, already outside Palestine, are looking to move outside the Arab world altogether. At all times, one of the key links among Palestinians is kinship. This is the reason why many contributions in this volume explore and examine the social and specifically the kin networks between Palestinians abroad and within the Palestinian territories and Israel as one of the factors facilitating return. On the one hand there are borders, on the other kin ties. These kin links often have an economic dimension, as economic actions are embedded within the kin networks. Embeddedness (Polanyi 1957) refers to the fact that diverse economic transactions are inserted into overarching social and political structures that affect their outcomes. Thus Palestinian economic transactions cannot be understood without referring to the social and legal status of the Palestinian communities. In other words, Palestinian choices on where and how to migrate reflect social links as much as economic logic.

The "Right of Return"

The study of borders, boundaries, social ties, and identities/belongings is an element of the sociology of return, part of the debate about the return of the Palestinian refugees. This debate is dominated by a legalistic discourse.

Dealing with a solution for the Palestinian refugee problem means to address not only their very just right to return, but also many factors which can influence their decision especially when the forced migration experience is extended over 60 years and a third and fourth generation is appearing in the host countries. Many unspoken and unthinkable issues are unexplored in the dominant discourse of right of return. Palestinian refugees interviewed in the Shaml center survey[3] have a much stronger feeling of nostalgia for the land of Palestine than for the people of Palestine. In interviews, refugees insisted on talking about property, the land, the Mediterranean Sea, al-Aqsa Mosque, or Deir Bor'om Church, and avoided the question of how they would live and with whom. I am not suggesting here the impossibility of the coexistence between Palestinian returnees and their Jewish neighbors, but the necessity of thinking the return not only in term of geography but also in term of social relations.

The right of return of Palestinian refugees to their place of origin is enshrined in four separate bodies of international law: humanitarian law, human rights law, the law of nationality as applied to state succession, and refugee law. Beyond these bodies of laws, which apply to all refugees in the world, the UN General Assembly specified the Palestinian case in Resolution 194, paragraph 11, December 11, 1948, which sets forth a framework for a solution to the problem of Palestinian refugees, including the possibility of return:

> *The refugees wishing to return to their homes and live at peace with their neighbors should be permitted to do so at the earliest practicable date, and that compensation should be paid for the property of those choosing not to return and for loss of or damage to property which, under principles of international law or in equity, should be made good by the governments or authorities responsible.* [4]

To understand the importance of the refugee issue to Palestinians, we must understand that the Palestinian nation and Palestinian nationalism as it exists today was born following the expulsion of over half the Palestinian

---

3 In 2004, the Palestinian Diaspora and Refugee Center (Shaml) conducted a survey among Palestinians living in Palestine/Israel which displays the variability of the transnational ties. As a team leader, I conducted this survey between January and October 2003. Five hundred sixty questionnaires were completed by refugees and non-refugees living in the camps and outside them.

4 See "194 (III). Palestine —Progress Report of the United Nations Mediator," The United Nations, December 11, 1948, (http://domino.un.org/unispal.nsf/0/c758572b78d1cd00852 56bcf0077e51a?OpenDocument).

population from their land in 1948, and that one of the fundamental aspects of Palestinian identity is "refugeehood." Such an understanding obliges us to address the problem of the Palestinian refugees as fundamental to any solution of the Palestinian-Israeli conflict.

There are five reasons for this: First, as long as the Israelis do not take into consideration what happened to the Palestinians in 1948 and the expulsion of the indigenous population from 78 percent of the land of historic Palestine, they will keep bargaining about the remaining 22 percent (the West Bank including East Jerusalem and the Gaza Strip). There is no solution to the land issue without coupling it with the refugee issue. This may be the reason why the Oslo Accords failed.

Second, resolving the refugee issue is not just a technical matter of absorption, nor is it a matter of reciting international law as if it were a self-implementing text. Rather, it involves deconstructing the Palestinian-Israeli conflict to its very premises, to understand how its causes led to a certain kind of colonial practice, and to recognize the need for a debate not just to understand, but also to acknowledge and accept, historic responsibility. This is the very precondition for true reconciliation and mutual forgiveness, as suggested by the late Edward Said (1999).

Third, irrespective of whether the final resolution of the Palestinian-Israeli conflict takes the form of a two-state or a bi-national state solution, the refugee issue cannot be considered secondary. The current intifada has revealed the importance of the refugees; they are the social and political actors most unable to bear the impasse in the Oslo process.

Fourth, beyond the moral and symbolic value of achieving a right of return, the right is useful in creating a framework for providing refugees with a choice between remaining in their host countries, returning to their places of origin or coming to a future Palestinian state (or third countries). The right of choice is a necessity for those who have, for more than half a century, been forced to live as aliens without basic rights in miserable camps and in states that have not always embraced them with open arms.

Finally, if the right of return and the right of choice is accepted, it will open many possibilities for the refugees to choose from. The movement of refugees depends on many factors related to their social, economic, and cultural identities. The return of refugees does not mean that the whole refugee community will move back to Israel. In almost all cases, the experience of refugees across the world shows that the number of those who return is less than those who choose other solutions. The Israeli phobia of a massive return is unjustified.

In her study of totalitarianism (1985:280), Hannah Arendt reminded us of "the decision of statesmen to solve the problem of statelessness by ignoring it." She insisted on the necessity of examining displacement through the prism of often xenophobic nation-states, and traced the political and symbolic logic that had the effect of "pathologizing" and even criminalizing refugees. The contemporary linkage that has been forged between Palestinian return and a disturbance of the regional order, especially in Israel, attests to the continuing relevance of Arendt's point.

Factors Influencing the Movement of Refugees

Many factors influence a refugee's decision whether to return or to choose another option. Understanding the likely patterns and pressures regarding Palestinian return cannot be achieved by focusing on macro processes of globalization or the operation of global markets according to neo-classical principles, but, rather, must be achieved by a sociological understanding of the political, social, and cultural attributes of the Palestinian people. One needs to examine elements related to the economic sociology of Palestinian refugees (and Palestinians abroad in general), both in the host country and in the country of return (the Palestinian Territories or Israel). Focusing on these elements should not overshadow other important factors.

For instance, geographical factors also influence refugees' decisions. Here it is worth noting the importance of Salman Abu Sitta's work (2001) in opening the debate concerning absorptive capacity of Israel. His efforts demonstrate that, after dividing Israel into three demographic areas, 68 percent of Israeli Jews are now concentrated in 8 percent of Israel and that the areas in and around the former Palestinian villages remain empty and could absorb returning refugees. For him, this empty rural area also corresponds to the original home location of the many rural refugees who are the majority of Palestinian refugees. However, it is important to ask if after so many years these refugees can still be considered peasants. The majority of them have become residents of big cites; it is thus pertinent to ask if they would accept to be resettled in their villages of origin. Those who became urban refugees were stripped of their ecological and sociological relationships. They may no longer identify with the land upon which they were working, which is what happened with Algerian refugees after independence (Lustick 1993:123). Moreover, according to the 2003 Palestinian Center for Policy and Survey Research (PSR) survey[5] in the Palestinian territories, the former dwellings

---

5   The PSR survey was conducted between January 16 and February 5, 2003, targeting 1,498 Palestinian refugee households distributed among 150 localities in the West Bank and Gaza Strip. See Results of PSR Refugees' Polls in the West Bank/Gaza Strip, Jordan, and Lebanon, PSR (http://www.pcpsr.org/survey/polls/2003/refugeesjune03.html).

of half of these refugees have been destroyed; more importantly, 40 percent declared themselves unwilling to return if a family home no longer exists. In other words, a right of return will not necessarily lead to an actual return; there are many intervening factors.

The return of Palestinian refugees is still closely connected with three elements: first, the right of return; second, the urban situation of the refugee camps; and, finally, the position of the Arab host countries. These three elements condition the degree to which the applicability of the right of return may be realized. It is also worth mentioning that many studies show that refugees have low expectations as to whether a political solution would allow most refugees to return. The 2003 PSR survey found that half the respondents accepted the idea that once a Palestinian state is established, the refugee issue will be postponed to an indefinite future.

Methodology for a Sociology of Return
This volume aims to be one of the first contributions to the sociology of the Palestinian return, moving away from many mythologies.[6] Many myths were circulated not only in popular thought but also within the scholarly community about the Palestinian refugee problem and their return. These myths must be researched and analyzed and perhaps debunked. The research agenda used in this book thus has three major features.

First, it is not a purely nation-centered approach to migration, nor a purely individual approach. As Elisabeth Longuenesse (2005:180) argues, since the 1980s, the study of the forced/voluntary/return migration makes less use of the nation-centered approach and focuses more on the individual benefits/disadvantages of the migrant in his/her relation to the family, to his/her solidarity networks, to his/her professional strategy, etc. Weak state control over the market, especially the labor market, is the primary reason and may be a consequence, but the market is not the only factor. The approach of this volume is to choose an individual approach in almost all of the chapters, and an intermediary level where the individual and nation-centered approaches are coupled in the chapters by Totry and Hanafi.

The second feature is linking voluntary migration with forced migration, as the frontier elaborated by the researcher is not always justifiable. New studies in transnationalism, diaspora, cultural studies, and hybridity suggest an analytical linkage between the migration experience, the exile experience, and return migration (see the chapters by Doraï and Hanafi). And, as

6   See Hanafi 1997, 2001, and 2002 for more elaboration.

Malkki notes (1995:514), both displacement and emplacement are seen as historical products and never-ending projects.

The third feature is a deconstruction of the notion of homeland and the form of the nation-state (see, for instance, the chapters by Parizot and Hanafi in this volume). Any thinking on the right and sociology of return should address the meaning and the validity of classical theories of sovereignty, democracy, state, and citizenship. Many functionalistic studies, as Malkki reminds us, have real consequences for the shape of intervention in refugee crises. For example, the functionalist visions of an identity that can only be whole when rooted in a territorial homeland reinforced the assumption that state sovereignty, as we know it, is part of the natural or necessary order of things (Malkki 1995).

This Collection

Sheerin al-Araj analyzes some parts of Shaml survey and examines different aspects of social capital that influence the decision of the refugees to return to al-Walaja village in Bethlehem District after the Green Line was established in 1949. She shows that in the case of al-Walaja the social ties between village dwellers and those living abroad remain stronger based on the identification with the land and with each other. She portrays the effort to retain a presence even on a remnant of the original village land. The presence of the al-Walaja Charity Society in Amman seems to be one of the most effective tools for maintaining ties between the al-Walaja refugee community in Jordan and al-Walaja village. However, she demonstrates an instrumentalization of this relationship, especially at the time of the election of the executive bureau of this society. Thus, one should not look to simple contact as the generator of a relationship.

Two case studies on the social and economic ties between Palestinians inside Israel with people in the Palestinian territories and abroad are very compelling in illustrating the impact of protracted rupture. Mary Totry's case study chooses a very interesting case to test the impact of the boundaries in identity construction and the emergence of the new Otherness. She studied how interactions evolved between the two parts of Barta'a village living on either side of the 1949 armistice line as a result of the division of the community between Israel and the West Bank, so that regional politics and legal issues affected the two parts of what was once a single kin group differentially. The village is now faced with a more terrible problem: the new Israeli wall cuts it off from the rest of the West Bank and circumscribes people's movements harshly. Cédric Parizot's study analyzes the trans-border exchanges that have evolved throughout the many political changes between the Bedouin in the Negev and their kin and network members, who became refugees in the West Bank, Gaza, and Jordan after 1948. He stresses how such encounters have linked cross-border populations through an intricate web of relations, while still fostering between them feelings of differences, power relations, and even antagonisms between groups. Occurring in an unequal framework of relationships, exchanges across borders are moments and places where people experience their differences and develop antagonisms. Indeed, while crossing borders, they rework and retain boundaries.

These two studies do not directly deal with a refugee population but the analysis that they provide is very important to grasp the role of protracted rupture in breaking down and restructuring kinship ties. Moreover, because they directly address the changing relationships between the different groups in the Palestinian populations, they emphasize the importance of seeing the refugees in close relationship and interaction with their environment and the people who remained in their place of origin. This indirect manner is thus crucial to understanding and predicting spatial movement among refugees.

Mohamed Kamel Doraï gives some insights into the efforts of the Palestinian refugees, especially since the beginning of the 1990s, to find a more congenial resting place than Lebanon with its restrictions. Their goal is to hold families together and to secure a reasonable income. Some have tried other Arab countries, notably Iraq, while others seek to move outside the Middle East, toward Europe. Contrary to the population in Palestine (refugees or not), transnational ties seems to be important in the case of the Palestinian refugees in Lebanon. For him the Palestinians do not use the same kind of transnational resources (i.e., economic, juridical, or educational) as the élites. Deprived of nationality and passport, they do not enjoy the same freedom of movement. Therefore, they use transnational family and village resources (mutual assistance, exchange of information) that facilitate migration. This know-how does not rely on an economic or juridical basis but on family and village-of-origin ties that cross national borders.

Tamara Tamimi presents a very interesting case on the negotiation of identity among American-born Palestinians who have returned with members of their families to live in the West Bank. Palestinians, like other diasporic communities, live in their host country while maintaining emotional, social, and often economic ties to their country of origin. The children of this population living in exile however, not having lived the history nor feeling the nostalgia or pain of loss associated with exile, inevitably possess an identity at variance and often in conflict with that of their parents. Palestinian-American returnees then, come to the West Bank to live knowing only what aspects of Palestinian identity, culture, and traditions were passed on to them by their parents while in the U.S. They also bring with them those aspects of American society which they have internalized and display as markers of their individual and group identity. Here tensions emerge between residents and returnees as each seeks to define the other based on an often limited knowledge of their respective societies. Tamimi offers us an excellent analysis of the cognitive and behavioral aspects of the Palestinian identity these particular returnees possessed while living in the U.S., and how the everyday reality of physically being in the homeland of their parents influenced or modified their identity and how it is expressed. If Palestinians are to return, the scenarios described here will become increasingly common.

This collection also examines the experience of the Palestinians who have already returned to the Palestinian territories. The work of Sari Hanafi evaluates the volume of the "return" to the Palestinian territories since the Oslo Agreements, and assesses the contribution of expatriates to the development of the Palestinian territories in terms of know-how and expertise. He compares two experiences of real and virtual return: the UNDP program that encourages repatriation called TOKTEN (The Transfer of Knowledge Through Expatriate Nationals) and the internet-based network, PALESTA (Palestinian Scientists and Technologists Aboard), which connects Palestinian scientists and professional expatriates to the Palestinian territories. He concludes with a critical assessment of the role of new media (like the internet) in facilitating the connectivity of the diaspora with the place of origin.

We hope that these papers will give the reader an understanding of the dilemmas of Palestinians expelled from their ancestral homes, or coping with divided villages, or traveling the world in search of a place to settle and raise a family. The processes related to the difficulties of crossing certain borders, the shifts in the boundaries themselves reflecting large-scale political conflicts, the place of these borders in the imagination of people as they seek shelter and try to reconstruct their lives, maintaining the significance of kinship and other direct personal relations over the broader abstract categories of identity politics, are all well illustrated in this collection.

Bibliography

Abu-Sitta, Salman. 2001. *The End of the Palestinian Israeli Conflict: From Refugees to Citizens at Home.* London: The Palestinian Return Center.

Arendt, Hannah. 1985. *Origins of Totalitarianism.* New York: Meridian.

Ghosh, Amitav. 1988. *The Shadow Lines.* UK: Penguin.

Hanafi, Sari. 1997. *Entre Deux Mondes: Les Hommes D'affaires Palestiniens de la Diaspora et la Construction de L'entité Palestinienne.* Cairo: CEDEJ.

————. 2001. *Hona wa Hunak: Nahwa Tahlil li al-'Alaqa bin al-Shatat al-Falastini wa al-Markaz* (Here and There: Towards an Analysis of the Relationship between the Palestinian Diaspora and the Center). Ramallah: Muwatin, Jerusalem: Institute of Jerusalem Studies (Arabic).

————. 2002. "Opening the Debate on the Right of Return," *Middle East Report,* 222:2–7.

Elisabeth Longuenesse. 2005. "Ouverture des Marchés et Mobilités Mrofessionnelles des Cadres." In Hana Jaber (dir.) and Françoise Metral, (dir.) *Mondes en Mouvements. Migrants et Migrations au Moyen-Orient au tournant du XXIe Siècle.* Beirut: IFPO.

Lustick, Ian. 1993. *Unsettled States, Disputed Lands: Britain and Ireland, France and Algeria, Israel and the West Bank-Gaza.* Ithaca, N.Y.: Cornell University Press.

Malkki, Liisa. 1995. Refugees and Exile: From 'Refugee Studies' to the National Order of Things," *Annual Review of Anthropology,* 24:495–523.

Polanyi, Karl. 1957. *The Great Transformation.* Boston: Beacon.

"Results of PSR Refugees' Polls in the West Bank/Gaza Strip, Jordan, and Lebanon," PSR (http://www.pcpsr.org/survey/polls/2003/refugeesjune03.html), accessed on July 18, 2003.

Said, Edward. 1999. "Truth and Reconciliation," *Al-Ahram,* 20 January.

United Nations. 1948. *Palestine: Progress Report of the United Nations Mediator, 194* (III), December 11. (http://domino.un.org/unispal.nsf/0/c758572b78d1cd0085256 bcf0077e51a?OpenDocument), accessed on: December 15, 2007.

Chapter 2

Social Ties between the People of al-Walaja Village at Home and Abroad

Sheerin al-Araj

Introduction

AL-WALAJA of today is a small Palestinian village situated about five kilometers to the northwest of Bethlehem and nine kilometers to the southwest of Jerusalem. It is surrounded on the east by the Gilo settlement (established in 1971), on the southeast by the Har Gilo settlement (established in 1972), while the Israeli bypass road 60 from Jerusalem to Gush Atzion settlements in Hebron circles the village like a noose. The 1948 war caused much damage to al-Walaja and most of its inhabitants were displaced. When the war stopped, the remnants of al-Walaja became a border village on the Jordanian side, since 75 percent of its original land lay across the Green Line.

When people returned to the remaining part of their village, they created New Walaja, where previously only a few families had lived, and took up the effort of rebuilding the village and reconstructing its society. The decision to return was not a collective one; each family came back on its own accord. But a new reality had been created that had far-reaching consequences for the composition of village society and by extension ordinary life and relationships among the villagers.

The geographic, social and political reality of al-Walaja continues to be in a state of flux. Having already suffered a major shock in 1948, the 1967 Israeli occupation subsequently also took a major toll on the village. Al-Walaja as I remember it was not the place it is today in many very obvious and intrusive ways. One hill has been confiscated for the Jewish settlement that straddles it, and adjoining territory is off limits to the villagers, having been cut off by a settlement bypass road. According to the local council figures, he current population of al-Walaja is around 1,695, divided into 300 families in 250 houses. The village has to contend with the rules of the Israeli occupation. It is deprived of basic services, and construction is forbidden among other restrictive measures that affect its development. Of course, many Walajans did not return, and the political center of gravity is now in the Walaja Cooperative Society in Amman.

This paper seeks to track the socio-political changes that al-Walaja's fate imposed upon it and to understand the impact of dispossession and exodus on the newly formed social structure. The study will examine the changes in al-Walaja's new community from different perspectives: socio-economic change in the context of family poverty, social adjustment, development in the status of women, social ties with the diaspora on different levels, and migration and return migration. The paper analyzes the effects of the new circumstances on the new societal composition, and how relationships developed as a result.

The relationships between Walajans in the village and in the diaspora remained strong despite separation, and I assume here that their sense of belonging to a shared place of origin is the main reason for this continuity. Normally, when people adapt to a new society as it evolves, they allow old social ties to fragment; this is social change. When the modes of human relationships change, so does social structure. Oral history and in-depth interviews were undertaken in order to depict the transformation in attitudes and in social structures in al-Walaja. It is the ideal tool for me since I am investigating personal, sensitive, and sometimes confidential information.

Socio-economic Changes in the Context of Family Desperation

Economic adjustment. Following the dispersion of al-Walaja's inhabitants and the subsequent return of some of them to New Walaja, the reconstruction of society began. This proved to be an extremely difficult task. Past criteria that had regulated life in the village had disappeared; what emerged was a completely new society in which people had known each other well but now also shared a joint history of displacement. Relations among people had changed and even past causes of disagreement had practically disappeared. Disagreements and quarrels over land became completely meaningless. The village square in the downtown where people used to meet ceased to exist and society became more and more individualized.

In addition, less agricultural land was available and agriculture ceased to be the main source of income. Available water resources diminished. Al-Walaja used to have many natural springs that made it a leading agricultural village, but Israeli forces had occupied a major part of the village and taken over most of the springs. Consequently, people could not just go back to farming. They had to head to nearby towns and cities such as Bethlehem, Beit Jala, and Jerusalem for work. Family members even went to Jordan, Syria, and Lebanon, leaving their relatives behind. Abu Mohammed said he had worked in Syria, Lebanon, and Jordan, as well as many parts of the West Bank, until the 1967 war broke out. When he returned to the village in the early 1970s, Abu Mohammed worked in Israel, as did most of al-Walaja's men at the time.

The disappearance of agricultural society in al-Walaja and the departure of more than three-quarters of its original inhabitants caused considerable change in the structure of society and social practices in the village. There was no formal structure for economic activities, and there was no interference from the state in these activities at all. As a whole they constituted an informal sector. Al-Walaja's people behaved in a remarkable fashion; they did not hold any governmental posts, mainly because they were landowners and not used to being part of a formal structure. They were used to a self-reliant, productive society and it determined their behavior.

Social adjustment. The extended family *(hamula)*[1] was the strongest social authority within the community. This social structure remained, influencing relations of people within and between *hamulas*. These influences are most apparent on significant occasions, like deaths and mourning rituals. The custom remains until today that a different *hamula* has to prepare food for the bereaved *hamula*. This is true for both the community in New Walaja and in Jordan where the majority of them reside now.

The election of the board for the Walaja Society in Amman also reflects the *hamula*'s influence. Elections are still decided according to the *hamula*

---

1   *Hamula* is an extended family made up of a number of households that share descent and hold the same family name.

structure, although there are notable changes from tradition. The *hamula*'s role in decision-making has diminished. The men, who in the past would have been considered "children" and a long way from being part of the decision making process, are now independent and solely responsible for their nuclear families. The gatherings of the old men in charge of making decisions in the *hamula* square no longer takes place, and decision-making these days is a much more difficult and complex process.

The social system built on the *hamula* witnessed sudden changes, mainly as a result of decisions by individuals to work in different places and in new vocations, in order to support their families. The increasing demands of life were the determining factor of that stage of their lives. At first, they tried to work the land, but it was obvious this would no longer yield enough income. Therefore, men abandoned agriculture and moved to work in other professions. Abu Mohammed, who used to be a farmer, became a construction worker. He said he learned the job from one of his father's friends, and he continued working in this field until retirement.

Hamula relations were also negatively affected by the 1948 war (*al-nakba*) and the dispossession of the Palestinian people. The practice of cohabiting extended families, which was a permanent feature at that time, was threatened. Many families formerly consisted of two brothers living together in one house along with their respective nuclear families. This is not the situation anymore; there are no houses large enough in al-Walaja to house them. The families had to separate, causing economic separation as well, and each head had to support his family on his own. This had a negative effect at the time, but some women said it was for the best.

"Why should we all stay together?" Um Ali said.

> There was no more land to be taken care of by all of us. In the old days, my father and my father-in-law, who was also my cousin, used to say that in order for us to protect the land and ensure a good income we needed to stay together. However, after the land was lost, there was no reason for all of us to stick together anymore.

Um Hussein said she had lived with the extended family, because her mother-in-law insisted that all her sons should live together. "We had to live with the family for 17 years after the *nakba*. The house was much smaller than it had been, and we were increasing in numbers. It was like pouring salt on our wounds," Um Hussein said.

Um Haitham, who was a child during the *nakba*, later got married to a man who owned a lot of land in New Walaja. Now that everyone works alone, she said, "I wish I had lived during those days when the people were working together all the time, my life would have been much easier."

Another change that occurred in the social structure of al-Walaja society was a substantial weakening of social solidarity and cooperative enterprise. People no longer assisted each other in agriculture or construction work. Um Ali remembered that before the *nakba* and emigration, people did not hire laborers to build their houses, something that changed after the *nakba*. She believed that the increasing responsibilities each individual had and the distance among people changed social relations. Earlier, she recalled, social solidarity was manifest in activities such as the harvest or house construction. The most difficult phase of the construction process is called *al-'aqd*, which means laying and cementing the roof of the house. All people used to help in this activity, and the helpers were called *awana*. The *awana* started to disappear and today is confined to close family members and close friends. Extended families no longer believe they have a social obligation to help each other, as was the case before the *nakba*. This feeling was augmented by the fact that members of the same extended family no longer lived together under the same roof and, as a result, they felt exonerated from any social commitment. Additionally, social authority as represented by the *sheikhs* of the extended families—and with it any kind of social punishment such as excommunication—ceased to exist.

The influx of people from al-Jora, a neighboring village, speeded up the pace of social change in al-Walaja. They bought land, built houses, mixed with al-Walajans and became part of the modern New Walaja society. Nevertheless, they are still called "al-Jorieh" after their original village, a name that has replaced the surnames of the newcomers.

Wedding ceremonies also witnessed change. Traditionally, the family of the groom cooked food and fed all the villagers, while the women carried food to the extended families, relatives, and friends. Even in times of disputes among people, women were obliged to feed every villager. Women also used to walk to the village square singing and ululating.

After the *nakba* such wedding ceremonies along with the extended families, as social phenomena, ceased to exist. Now the ceremonies are arranged in a much simpler fashion, and only the ones attending the party get food. Social visits became rare because of the long distances separating houses. Um Ali says she lived with her husband in a place called Wadi Halas to the east of al-Walaja, while her family lived to the west of the village and walking to her family's house "took hours." She used to visit her family only once a month.

Changes in the status of women. The status of women has changed drastically. They became active participants in the decision-making process in the family and more efficient in household administration. The woman had to shoulder huge responsibilities, as many men and husbands were either killed or imprisoned by the Israeli or Jordanian armies. Women were importantly responsible for bringing water from the springs to the home, an important and, sometimes, hazardous job. Um Ali says she was almost shot by Israeli soldiers when trying to fetch water from one of the springs. It was these changes that forced people over time to change their behavior and eventually led them to accept different norms. For instance, women started delivering in hospitals instead of at home.

Women also obtained the right to education. Many girls from the village began to attend schools in nearby towns and cities. This right was obtained after significant pressure from the older women, who had not been allowed to attend school in the old village. Um Hussein said, "When my daughter reached the age of six, she was supposed to start school, but her father did not allow her." The following year, another girl, who was Abu Mohammed's daughter, reached the age of six and her mother insisted on educating her. Dispute between the parents reached to the point where Abu Mohammed's wife threatened to leave the house with her daughter if the father did not allow the girl to attend school, so eventually he consented. Um Hussein then coerced her husband in the same manner, and both girls started school in Beit Jala that year. They used to go together to Beit Jala to attend school there. Eventually, Aysha, Um Hussein's daughter, stopped attending school after 6th grade because she had to go to Bethlehem to do so, and the father would not permit that. Fatima, Abu Mohammed's daughter, continued her school education and managed to finish her first year of college. After her mother passed away, she had to quit. Many girls from this generation pursued an education. There are now a few female teachers, nurses, and even a lawyer. Those who did not attend school attended UNRWA-sponsored training programs that were offered to refugee women in neighboring camps.

Social Relationships with the Diaspora

Relationships between Palestinians in al-Walaja and those in the diaspora were maintained. Palestinians who were expelled from the village to neighboring Arab countries and refugee camps returned occasionally to al-Walaja, but were unable to settle there again either due to the difficult life in the village or because they had already established themselves in exile. At any rate, they still managed to return to the village on joyful or sorrowful occasions.

Such visits were curtailed by the 1967 war, although they resumed later at a slower pace.

Relationships with first-degree relatives in the diaspora differ from those with more distant ones. To get a clearer picture of the socioeconomic transnational relationships between al-Walajans, each will be considered separately.

First-degree relatives. Fieldwork results reveals that on average two people from every nuclear family live in the diaspora. They work, study, or are married outside the country. Economic and social relationships among family members are very strong. Distances play a small role and people tend to ignore the geographical separation in their answers. More than 95 percent of the young men working abroad send money to help their families in the village and vice versa. In spite of their dire economic situation, families in al-Walaja still manage to send money to their relatives abroad.

Like all Palestinians, the people of al-Walaja were greatly affected by the two *intifadas* that broke out in 1987 and 2000, but in spite of them, they never refrained from sending assistance to relatives abroad. In many instances, more than 50 percent of the people would refer to the absent person as part of the household, even if that person had been away for several years. They would insist they be part of the decision-making process in the family and not just a provider.

In order to inquire about the strength of these relationships, we asked about the frequency of phone calls and found out that, in most cases, they occurred at least once a week. Through these calls, both parties exchange ideas on various issues and take important decisions as if they were living together.

The study also reveals that a good number of al-Walajans living in the diaspora own land and a small number of them own homes in al-Walaja and are planning to return to them some time in the future. They also regularly visit the village. It was discovered that landowners are planning to return some day to al-Walaja and that those sharing agricultural land also share its profit. Equally interesting is the fact those who are now living in al-Walaja and are taking care of land they do not own, acknowledge that they are simply taking care of it until their rightful owners return. The owners abroad pay their share to cultivate and preserve the land.

Second-degree relatives. Social relationships between second-degree relatives (aunts, uncles and their offspring) of the same family are relatively strong. It seems that borders do not affect them and most of the relatives know a lot about each other, visiting each other on social occasions, such as weddings and, definitely, funerals. A big majority of the interviewees said that it is a must to be at the funerals of second-degree relatives, but it is mainly men who are expected to attend. Women are rarely required to attend, unlike the case with funerals of first-degree relatives where all are expected to attend. Such relationships are also considered important from a socio-religious perspective. Kinship visits, for example, continue to take place to this day in spite of distance and other obstacles. There is also a high level of cooperation among relatives in solving family problems. For instance, almost all relatives of the same family help each other in paying blood money, due when a member of the family kills a person from another family by mistake and is imprisoned. The payment is enough to secure the prisoner's release.

Relationships among men and women retain their traditional form. Men still fulfill their socio-economic duty in assisting women financially when needed, inquiring about their health, and offering them gifts on feasts and other occasions.

Similarly, relationships among the young are strong, which are strengthened by the use of email and cellular phones. Now, young men and women in al-Walaja have access to electronic means to contact friends and relatives abroad. Even relatives from the same family, who never had the chance to visit al-Walaja, can now establish relations with relatives in the village. Furthermore, economic relations are enhanced. More than half of the people interviewed expressed the fact that the exchange of gifts has become more common, and financial assistance, especially to women, has become more frequent. Kinship relations obligate male members of the family to offer financial assistance to aunts and nieces. Men could never shun this responsibility, even if they were financially insolvent.

However, at the level of third-degree relatives, social relationships are declining and almost disappearing. Except during very formal occasions, phone contacts replace social visits. For instance, most people visit each other only for funerals and less for weddings. Such a weakening in social relationships does not create feelings of guilt in the individual. In fact, some may not know the names of other family members. Fieldwork reveals that relationships are strongest among family members of the same age. They spend time together and correspond with each other.

We found out that a good number of those who returned to Palestine after the Gulf War or the signing of the Oslo Accords have maintained third-degree relationships with other family members. There are regular contacts among them, especially after the eruption of the second *intifada* in 2000. This *intifada* has a very significant influence on social and economic relationships at different levels, because social visits are no more possible. As a result, there has been a considerable rise in phone calls to family members as those living abroad regularly call their relatives in Palestine, especially after the Israeli army began their incursions into various Palestinian cities and villages.

The Israeli parliament has passed a law which prevents any Palestinian or Arab Israeli from marrying someone who does not hold a legal document to stay in the West Bank or in Israel. Thus,

> *The only procedure available to a person not registered in the population registry to be allowed to live lawfully in the occupied territories is family unification. A request for family unification may be submitted only by a first-degree relative of the applicant who holds residency status in the occupied territories. Most requests are submitted for residents' wives who are of Palestinian origin and Jordanian nationals. The large number of families in which one spouse is a resident and the other a foreigner results from the continuing ties of residents with the Palestinian diaspora and from Israel's policy, which forced residents to find work and to study abroad, and to establish a family outside the occupied territories.* ("Separation of Families")

Institutionalizing ties. Cooperative relationships between Palestinians living in al-Walaja and those abroad were institutionalized by the creation of the Cooperative Society which was established in Amman, Jordan, in order to cater for the interests of al-Walajans in Jordan. Palestinians residing in al-Walaja village pay a nominal membership fee to the society and participate in the election of its administrative board. The relationship between al-Walajans in Palestine and Jordan was used to play out the power struggle that had existed among families before the *nakba* and later re-appeared in different ways. The election process is just a reflection of the change in power relations between families after the exodus. Now the relationships are very much affected by the occupation. For example, members of al-Araj *hamula* are fighting among themselves over one of them who was a collaborator with the Israeli army. The argument led to a division in the *hamula* in al-Walaja and outside. The same division over the same problem is happening in different places in the world, mainly in Amman and the West Bank. It indicates the strength of such relations between these people.

The cooperative society replaced the village square system that was dominant before 1948. It is the place where different *hamulas* convene. It is also regarded by the people of al-Walaja as a compensatory center that brings them together and protects them from further dispersion. The society represents all the *hamulas* of al-Walaja, who compete for leadership roles.

Such cases of relationships and communication reveal a lot concerning the relationships of Palestinians in al-Walaja. In times of need and hardship, refugees from al-Walaja living in neighboring Arab countries and West Bank refugee camps collect financial aid to assist those living in al-Walaja now. Such magnanimity was displayed when many men who had been working inside Israel had to quit their jobs, due to Israeli-imposed closures.

Membership in the society is open to anyone from the village no matter where she/he resides. Everyone is supposed to pay an annual fee to use the services and the facilities, which include the celebration hall where members get cheap rates for weddings, and which they can use for funerals for free. The society also offers a few medical services. The management is elected by the general assembly, which includes all fee-paying members, and thus, during elections, all fees are usually paid. The election is based on the *hamula* system whereby each *hamula* presents its candidates for the council. All kinds of different coalitions between families and even influential individuals enter into the process.

People who live in the Palestinian territories can also vote if they pay the required fee. For example, I pay my fee every year and maintain my membership. My brother, who lives in Amman, was the head of the management council a few times, as was my uncle. They usually contact me to pay my dues and send me the legal authorization for a proxy vote. This occurs with most everyone who lives in al-Walaja; their relatives from Jordan who run the society make sure they are voting. However, the relatives are actually the ones who decide to whom the votes go. I hardly know the other candidates and I presume most Walaja residents do not know them either, so our relatives use our votes in their coalitions.

Another important tradition that al-Walajans have preserved is the family fund. Each family sets up its own fund to cover the expenses of social duties or commitments and to meet the economic needs of the family and the village. Money from the family fund has been utilized in building al-Walaja's school and in constructing roads. The money is also used to help family members in need.

Endogamy (marriage between members of the same family) is a common practice. There have been cases in which members of one family living in al-Walaja married from the same family abroad. In each extended family, there is at least one case of such a marriage. Such marriages are an example of distinguished social relationships, and they are not solely confined to relatives in the second degree, but also include relatives from the third degree.

There are cases in which people from al-Walaja had to leave the village for marriage, most of them women, since it is customary that the bride should move to her groom's home. However, there have been a small number of cases where the groom left to live in his bride's place of residence. Marriages seem sustainable, as no divorce case has been registered, in spite of the increasing number of such marriages.

Migration and Return Migration

According to the field study, the sense of belonging and connection among al-Walajans is very strong and genuine, irrespective of their age, sex, education, or social background. They define themselves as refugees in Palestinian territories. They regard the original al-Walaja, occupied by Israel in 1948, as their homeland, and they feel they have to return to it one way or another.

The study also revealed that a large number of al-Walaja's residents carry a Palestinian passport. Some hold the Israeli travel document ("laissez-passer"), and a few prefer to hold a Jordanian passport. Some have left the village to live in Jerusalem in order to maintain their Jerusalem identity cards, since the Israeli authorities are now confiscating identity cards from Palestinians who do not actually reside within the borders of Jerusalem. We met and interviewed people from al-Walaja who had left the village to live in Jerusalem, and in some cases all family members were obliged to leave al-Walaja and live in Jerusalem. All of them consider al-Walaja as their permanent address and Jerusalem as a temporary one.

Very few first-degree relatives of the village residents live in the diaspora, which indicates that small families usually tend to stay together in one place. We also found that often more than one family live in the same house, since the Israeli authorities do not grant construction permits. This is one reason why members of the same family have stayed together and hence, social proximity in the village has become very high. Al-Walajans strive to adjust their lives and to cope with the oppressive Israeli rules and regulations in order to protect their land, their identity, and themselves.

Al-Walajans residing outside Palestine are the least fortunate. The largest number of them live in Jordan and suffer most in comparison to those who live in other places. Many of them live below the poverty line. A good many al-Walajans currently live in the Gulf countries, mainly in the United Arab Emirates. Others are scattered between the U.S. and Europe.

Evidently, al-Walajans have a strong inclination to remain in their village, except when there is a strong case for their departure. In an attempt to examine the journey to and from al-Walaja, we discovered that all those who had left did so in spite of themselves. The main cause of emigration was the 1948 *nakba*. People left for Jericho, Jerusalem, Beit Jala, and various refugee camps in Palestine. Some returned to their village, and the wave of return persists until this day. The more fortunate saved some money and returned to the village, where they built their own houses and settled down. Most of the returnees came back from Jordan and the Gulf countries in the 1960s. Some others returned in the aftermath of the Gulf War and the signing of the Oslo Accords. The total number of returnees amount to 5 percent of the current population of al-Walaja. Men returned mainly for education and work, while women returned because of marriage.

The impression I got from my personal visits to Jordan is that all homes I visited kept some sort of symbol for Palestine, such as a map of Palestine or a picture of al-Haram al-Sharif. Most maintained that such symbols are "what we can possess from the lost homeland." In a few cases, one person in the family was responsible for collecting these items. In other cases, pictures and symbols of Palestine would be among a multitude of other pictures of pop stars and cars that teenagers hung in their rooms. Their attachment to the symbols signifies their attachment to their place of origin, and many of these people will consider returning to al-Walaja when it is legally possible.

Some of the residents may return despite their awareness of the difficulties they will encounter. Those who were asked to express their opinion about the prospect of return to the village said that it would not be easy to adjust to a new kind of life in al-Walaja. According to them, returnees usually face problems finding work and suitable accommodation. There is also the problem of adapting to the people in the village. "To settle anew in the village is not that easy," is a commonly stated comment. Nevertheless, the inclination to return is strong in spite of the difficulties. Besides, those who have returned have told others who wish to return about the hardships, and there are few illusions about what it might mean to return home after such a long absence.

Indeed, returnees expressed satisfaction about their lives in al-Walaja. Talking to them we could sense a feeling of nostalgia for a past that now exists only in their minds. The people we questioned were more than delighted to offer personal accounts of their life in exile and in Palestine. They talked about the severe Israeli occupation and the way it has damaged their life and put an end to their ambitions. They said that diaspora life was much easier, and they remembered the liberty they possessed to move from one place to another without any restrictions.

There were also differences among the returnees themselves that emerged during the interviews. Many complained about life under Israeli occupation. Those who protested most were the young; the old complained but were more realistic in accepting and adapting to the new lifestyle.

It was also clear that most refugees did not believe there would be a solution that would enable them to return home. Such a lack of trust might be called "realism," and we can say all refugees enjoy a sense of political realism that surpasses even that of political researchers and decision makers. However, I believe such realism stems from frustration and internal defeat more than from a reasonable understanding of the nature of the Palestinian-Israeli conflict.

On the one hand, it seemed to me that the majority of the Palestinian refugees believed (out of desperation) that a substitute for return would come in the form of compensation, or a return to the territories under Palestinian control, or resettlement in some Arab country. Other refugees expressed an earnest desire to return, even though some preferred to maintain economic relations with al-Walaja while staying in their new places of residence. They preferred to keep and administer the land they owned from a distance.

Conclusion

In 1948, the *nakba* uprooted the Palestinians from their homes. They lost their land, which was their main source of wealth and pride, as well as social prestige. As a result, they became refugees on other people's land, both inside and outside of what was left of Palestine. They have become strangers in their own home. This uprooting affected all aspects of life; in particular, it affected the traditional social structure of Palestinian communities, regardless of where they have come from or where they have moved.

The ongoing process of social structure formation among the refugees has re-established old social ties and resulted in the formation of new ones, whether among themselves or with people in the host countries. This paper focused on the process whereby a community re-emerged. In some ways, this community maintained the traditional social structure of the original one, and in other ways the reconstruction of the community established distinct forms of structure based on the new economic, political, and social realities. The previous social structure influenced the construction of the community in the new setting. Farmers either turned into people without land or lost their means of livelihood.

Some Palestinians made a personal decision to live where they most wanted, disregarding difficulties, and this made them regroup with their kin and other members of the same village instead of staying in refugee camps that had been set up by UNRWA.

Based on the limited information we have about the construction of communities in the host countries, it seems that Palestinian refugees in Jordan adjusted themselves to their new surroundings. They managed to create new social settings and meet their needs as a social structure, as evidenced by the establishment of new forms of social organization such as al-Walaja coopera-tive society in Amman.

Many other similar societies were established for different Palestinian vil-lages. Walking around Amman one sees the names of Palestinian villages and cities all around the city, such as Haifa or Safad and so forth. Sometimes families from one of the cities or villages have their own place, which is not necessarily a society but rather something like a *diwan* (meeting house), which is also a location for the social gathering of a certain *hamula*.

The establishment of economic and social relations within the new envi-ronment represents another model of new social ties formed in the host communities. One remarkable behavior of Palestinian refugees can be seen in the naming of their new businesses or streets after the places they had come from; they want anything to be named after their villages or famous sites in them, like al-Walaja Vegetable Market in Bethlehem, or al-Walaja Supermarket in Amman. This is another way of showing the connection to their land and gives an indication of their feeling toward their cause as refu-gees. This phenomenon needs careful study to discover what significance it might have if it came to a choice to return.

Walajans realize the importance of education and they maintain a high percentage of educated people in the village, both men and women. Surprisingly, women have become more educated over time, hence improv-ing their social status in the community. Subsequently, men's attitude toward women has changed dramatically mainly due to their dependency on the help women provide in severe circumstances. Education contributed immensely to this change as well. Women's attitudes toward themselves and their living conditions pose a serious challenge toward existing norms, which had undermined them as contributors to society. A similar development has taken place regarding marriage arrangements.

The people of al-Walaja found themselves in a different structure and while they retained many of their existing social patterns, unconsciously they also formed something new. Religion was an important factor to bind them all to each other.

The feelings of the people toward their lost homeland are very strong. In answer to the direct question, "Would you go back?" the great majority answered, "Yes, we will go back whenever possible." It is an answer in keep-ing with the new ties they have formed over the years.

In the end, taking into consideration the severe measures the Israeli occu-pation is taking against al-Walaja, it is very difficult to predict what is going to happen in the future to these people who have tried very hard to maintain their identity or at least their belonging. The segregation wall and the confiscation of more land in the village in order to build a new settlement around the village will complete the circle around al-Walaja village on three sides: northern, eastern, and western, and will limit contact with the village. Consequently, inhabitants of al-Walaja are becoming prisoners and refugees in their own homeland.

Bibliography

"Separation of Families: The Prohibition on Family Unification in the Occupied Territories," *B'etsilim* (http://www.btselem.org/English/Family_Separation/Index.asp) accessed on: December 15, 2007.

Chapter 3
Changing Realities and Changing Identities
Case Study of the Divided Village of Barta'a

Mary Totry

Introduction

Socio-political borders create new realities that shape new political, cultural, and social identities. This paper aims to examine the political orientation and collective identities of the Palestinians in Israel and the West Bank through the case study of Barta'a village. It first traces the political history and identity formation of people from this originally homogeneous village, suggesting that the times are at least as important as origins in shaping people's outlook. It then reports on the "collective identities" found in this complex community.

This study aims to examine the "divergence thesis" and the "convergence thesis" concerning the differences that were developed between the two parts of Barta'a by making systematic comparisons between them during four periods: the separation years 1949–67, the "reunion" years 1967–87, the first *intifada* 1987–95, and finally the Oslo process and the second *intifada*. This research is based on data collected during six months (February–July) in 1995 and a follow-up period (November–December) in 2003. We held structured interviews with residents from both parts of the village, the *mukhtar*[1] of each, as well as a number of community activists. During the

---

1 The *mukhtar* (village head) is a representative figure who mediates with the authorities and fulfills various roles.

follow-up research, we held interviews with residents from East Barta'a and with the head of the village council.

Barta'a Divided: One Village, Two Worlds

Barta'a, west of Jenin, was one of three villages that were divided in 1949 between Jordan and Israel as a result of the Rhodes Armistice Agreement.[2] The Israeli and Jordanian negotiators declared the valley crossing the village as the armistice line (known later as the Green Line) disregarding the trauma caused to thus-divided families.[3]

All the residents of Barta'a were Muslim members of the Kabha clan (*hamula*). They shared a common heritage, language, religion, culture, and to some extent a national consciousness. After the division, the Israeli half became known as "West Barta'a" and the West Bank half as "East Barta'a." Up until 1967, contacts were prevented between the two parts of the village. As a result, they developed as two distinct communities. When they were "reunited" in 1967 by the Israeli occupation of the West Bank, their political status, as far as citizenship was concerned, did not allow them to reestablish the unity they had earlier. During the first twenty years of the "reunion," they had minimal interaction. The first *intifada* (1987) highlighted the differences in their political orientation by resurrecting the old Green Line that separated them. According to the Oslo II Accord signed in 1995, East Barta'a became part of area "C" (under Israeli authority) until a final agreement could be reached between Israel and the Palestinian National Authority (PNA). However, the outbreak of the second *intifada* (2000) and the construction of the "Apartheid Wall" in 2002 created a new reality. East Barta'a and other border villages became part of the "closed areas"[4] imprisoned between the Green Line and the Wall and disconnected both from the Palestinian territories and Israel. Their future is still vague. Will they be annexed to Israel and given Israeli citizenship as was the case for their brethren in West Barta'a? Will East Barta'ans, who have defined themselves as Palestinians, start defining themselves differently?

When the West Bank was annexed to the Hashemite Kingdom after the creation of Israel, the 600 residents of East Barta'a were given Jordanian

---

2 The other two were Baqa, slightly to the south, and Beit Safafa, near Jerusalem.

3 Jordan handed over the Triangle area (22 villages with 30,000 residents) to Israel. Israel annexed them as the Palestinian population was too small and too powerless to be able to dilute the Jewish character of the state.

4 The population of Palestinians in these areas is 17,000 residing in 64 communities along the Green Line.

citizenship while the 400 residents of West Barta'a were given Israeli citizenship. Until 1955, the *mukhtar* continued to run both sides of the village and was officially permitted to travel both to Amman and to Tel Aviv.[5] Subsequently, a *mukhtar* was appointed to run each side of the village.

The village's only mosque fell in East Barta'a, while the village school, the cemetery and the water well were located in West Barta'a. The children of East Barta'a had to study in rented rooms until two schools were built for them: one for boys in 1953 and another for girls in 1956. West Barta'ans had to pray in a private house until they built a mosque of their own just as East Barta'ans had to establish a cemetery. At first, the two sides shared the water well: women from the western side pumped water during the morning hours while women from the eastern side pumped water only during afternoon hours. In the early 1960s, the Jordanian authorities set up a water reservoir to prevent any contact between the two communities. Land was the major problem to both parts of the village. Israel confiscated most of the land on its side and regarded land that belonged to easterners as "absentee property,"[6] while Jordan considered land that belonged to the westerners as enemy property (Kabha 1986).

Although crossing the border was forbidden, some infiltrated at night to check on their relatives. During the first decade of separation, West Barta'a was isolated from the outside world and suffered from food shortage.[7] The residents of the eastern part used to smuggle them some of their basic needs. This was the case until 1956 when the first clash erupted between the Israeli and the Jordanian army and developed into a serious confrontation. Residents from both villages fled and hid in caves nearby. When they returned, they found a three-kilometer marked border across the valley creating a new reality. Crossing from one side to the other was totally prohibited. A Jordanian police station was placed in the center of East Barta'a and anyone who was caught crossing the border was imprisoned (Kabha 2003). Since then the official separation was finalized and the two parts lost contact with each other. Nevertheless, the two parts tried to stay informed about each other as best they could despite the severe restrictions. They held their wedding and funeral ceremonies near the border so their relatives across the border could watch them from afar.

---

5 He resided in East Barta'a and was given Israeli citizenship until he was exiled to the Jordanian Desert.

6 1,462 dunams were considered "absentee property."

7 Anyone who wanted to get out of the village had to apply for a special permit from the Ara'a military station located at a distance of 7 kilometers (Kabha 1986).

The "Divergence Thesis" and "Convergence Thesis"

Two conflicting theses conceptualize the similarities and differences in the political orientation of the two Palestinian communities. The "convergence" thesis posits that in their collective identification the Palestinians in Israel would stress their Palestinian national identity rather than their Israeli civic identity, and that the political orientation they would adopt is similar to that of the Palestinians in the West Bank and Gaza Strip. The "divergence" thesis, on the other hand, points to increasing differences between the two communities and postulates a separate collective identity for the Palestinians in Israel.

That these two theoretical approaches arrive at opposite conclusions stems from the way they define the role of citizenship. According to the "convergence" thesis, the Palestinians in Israel do not attach much significance to their Israeli citizenship. The "divergence" thesis asserts the contrary even though the Palestinians are well aware that their Israeli citizenship does not grant them full equality compared to the Jews. The two theses, moreover, conceive of the Israeli democratic system in different ways. Benvenisti (1987, 1989) sees Israel as a "Herrenfolk democracy," whereby one ethnic group takes up a status of full superiority to the detriment of the civic rights of all other groups. Smooha (1990), on the other hand, defines Israel as an "ethnic democracy," a system that grants democratic rights to all its citizens but at the same time demands explicit ethnic dominance for one group, whose structured superior status is institutionalized.

Palestinian Citizens in Israel and Palestinian Citizens in the Hashemite Kingdom of Jordan: 1948–1967

The political separation in 1948 caused structural, economic, demographic, and social changes in the two Palestinian societies—those who became Israeli citizens and those who became Jordanian citizens. As a result of being annexed to two different political entities, they began to adapt to their new realities and developed their own distinct characteristics.

The establishment of Israel caused major changes in the social, economic and political structure of the Palestinian society in Israel. The Palestinians who remained in their homeland became, overnight, a minority in a state that fought and continued to fight their own nation.[8] They were compelled to depend on it economically, structurally, politically, and legally. They were separated from the rest of the Palestinian nation and from the Arab world

---

8   160,000 out of 900,000 Palestinians remained in Israel; the rest became refugees in the West Bank, Gaza Strip, and the neighboring countries.

of which they were culturally and socially a part (Kabha 1986). Bishara (1993) claims that the Palestinians who remained in Israel were a vanquished minority, the periphery of the original Palestinian community: a rural community lacking political, cultural, and religious leadership.

Israel imposed a policy of "control" to restrict them (Lustick 1980). On one hand, Palestinian localities were put under direct military administration until 1966. The military administration limited the freedom and the movement of the Palestinian population. It was replaced later by a subtle machinery of surveillance. During this period the majority of the traditional leadership[9] was co-opted while political activists were harassed and repressed.[10] Official policy encouraged clan and religious factionalism (Christians, Druze, Bedouin, and non-Bedouin Muslims) to inhibit the rise of nationalism and concerted political resistance. On the other hand, Palestinians were given Israeli citizenship and continued to have separate community institutions (under the strict supervision of the state) and separate identities.[11] They were also extended several welfare services.[12]

During the first decade, Israel confiscated most of the Palestinians' land leading to a major change in their occupational structure. Since the mid-1950s Palestinians underwent a process of proletarization: they deserted agriculture and turned to wage labor, thus gradually becoming dependant on the Israeli labor market. This was due to the massive land confiscations and the increasing demand for Palestinian labor. As a result, there was a significant rise in the living standard of most Palestinians (Rosenfeld 1959).

Smooha (1989) claims there has been a cultural change amidst the young Palestinian generation as a result of their interaction with the Jewish society. They became bilingual and bicultural, becoming thus a distinct Palestinian segment. Their constant interaction with Jewish society began to weaken their cultural and religious tradition (Kabha 1986). Nevertheless, the process was not able to abolish all traditional patterns, and social and religious traditions persisted (Lehman-Wiltzig 1993).

The Palestinians in Israel began gradually to crystallize their orientation towards the state, the Jewish majority, and their status as a minority. They realized that they had become a permanent minority in Israel. During that period

---

9   The *mukhtars* and the heads of the *hamulas*.

10 Communist activists were harassed and occasionally imprisoned. Toward the 1965 Knesset elections, an the nationalist Arab list "al-Ard," the first predominantly Arab party, attempted to run for elections, but it failed.

11 Israel did not enforce a cultural assimilation policy on the Palestinians so as to preserve the unique ethno-national Jewish majority.

12 Health, education, social security benefits, and Histadrut (trade union) protection.

"Arabism" not "Palestinianism" was the major component in their national identity inspired by the accelerating "Pan Arabism" of the Nasser regime in Egypt. They perceived themselves as part of the Arab world but at same time they wanted to be integrated, not assimilated, in Israel (Osaski-Lazar 1990).

Smooha (1991) claims the Palestinians gradually learnt the rules of the Israeli democratic system and began to test its tolerance. Bishara (1993), on the other hand, claims that the Palestinians' aspirations at that time were set no higher than to achieve security rather than equality. They adopted "positive political" behavior[13] in order not to be expelled from their homeland. This "positive" behavior did not indicate their willingness to integrate, but their acceptance of reality out of fear.[14] Palestinians from all political streams identified with Nasser and Pan Arabism, which showed their alienation from the state.

The status of Palestinians in Israel was inferior to that of the Jews. Being part of the Palestinian nation and the Arab world they were regarded by the Jewish majority and the state apparatus as potentially disloyal (fifth column) and hence excluded from military service. They were not allowed to integrate in different spheres of Israeli society. Although they enjoyed limited social and economic mobility, they were not represented in most national offices (Smooha 1989).

Palestinians in the West Bank, who were occupied by Transjordan in 1948,[15] did not undergo a demographic upheaval.[16] They preserved their social institutions, religious and social leadership as well as their traditional linguistic and cultural patterns. Although they were separated from their brethren in Israel, they had free access to the entire Arab world. They moved in large numbers seeking education and job opportunities. Many of them never returned to the West Bank.

Jordan granted full individual civil rights to the Palestinians in the West Bank,[17] but forced them to assimilate by denying them cultural, political, and

---

13 Voting for Zionist parties, not opposing the discrimination to which they were subjected.

14 During that time the army and security organs mediated between the state and the Palestinian population.

15 Annexing the West Bank put an end to the UN partition plan to establish a Palestinian state alongside Israel. The Hashemites opposed an independent Palestine and cooperated with the Zionist Movement to expand their kingdom to the West Bank. In 1950, King Abdullah I changed the name of the state to the Hashemite Kingdom of Jordan (Shlaim 1988).

16 300,000 refugees who were expelled from their homeland during the war sought shelter in the West Bank, while 200,000 sought shelter in Transjordan.

17 Two thirds of Jordan's population is Palestinian. Since the annexation of the West Bank was not internationally recognized, Jordan had to consolidate its rule over the Palestinians to prevent resistance (Smooha 1991).

administrative autonomy. As individuals they were entitled to vote, to travel, to own property, and to engage in economic activities, but were not allowed to establish political parties, run a separate system of education, and form a separate national identity. They were treated with suspicion: they could serve in the civil administration and security forces, but were informally hindered from getting top-ranked and sensitive positions (Smooha 1991). However, they did not oppose the discriminatory policy against them because they were, as were Palestinians elsewhere, shocked, confused, and too weak to resist. They were also enthusiastic Pan Arabists, believing that the liberation of Palestine could be secured only through Arab unity. They thus did not try to form a separate Palestinian identity and sought to cooperate with Arab governments.

Jordan did not invest much in the West Bank which remained underdeveloped. Palestinians who sought better opportunities had to emigrate to the East Bank or to the Gulf states. The West Bank remained exclusively a Palestinian territory and preserved its character. Only in the late 1950s did the Palestinians start to develop a separate identity from the Arab world. The trauma of 1948 faded, educational and living standards improved, and new organizations emerged. Many Palestinians felt they could no longer rely on the Arab countries to defeat Israel and formed their own guerilla organizations.

West and East Barta'a: 1949–1967

During the British Mandate, Barta'a was underdeveloped compared to the nearby villages. Located on hills and far from the main road, it was neglected and its infrastructure remained underdeveloped. Its residents lived mainly on traditional agriculture (subsistence crops), cutting wood for coal, and on livestock.

After the division, an Israeli military administration was imposed on West Barta'a.[18] A significant part of their land was confiscated[19] in the first decade leading to a considerable worsening of their economy. The village suffered from large-scale unemployment and some of its residents engaged in smuggling across the border. Nevertheless, agriculture continued to be the main the source of income for most of the residents.

---

18 They were totally isolated from their nearby surroundings, forbidden to communicate with their relatives across the border, and restricted from having contacts with the neighboring Palestinian villages in Israel.

19 Barta'a had 7,059 dunams in 1948. Israel confiscated more than two thirds of its land, leaving 1,005 dunams for agriculture and 808 for construction (Kabha 1986).

In the mid-1950s the military authorities started to ease up on issuing work permits to Palestinian workers, thus initiating the proletarization process. Some of the residents of West Barta'a entered the Israeli labor market,[20] leading to a significant rise in their living standard. They built new houses and changed their consumption patterns and lifestyle. The changes were mainly reflected on the individual level, and there were almost no significant changes in the village infrastructure. The internal roads and the road connecting the village with the main road remained unpaved. Most of the villages near Jewish localities were connected to the electricity grid in the 1960s and their residents enjoyed running water. Barta'a, being small and remote, was neglected (it was connected to the electricity grid only in 1981). In the late 1950s, West Barta'ans began to enjoy some social benefits, and the workers' admittance to the Histadrut improved their status and their rights at work (Kabha 1986).

In the 1960s, two rooms were added to the existing school, an elementary school serving both boys and girls. Students who wanted to continue their studies had to walk an hour each way to nearby villages. The educational system for the Palestinians in Israel was not well organized and the curriculum ignored their national identity (Mar'i 1976).

Although the military administration restricted the contacts of West Barta'ans with the outside world in the first two decades, it was hard to discern the presence of the military in the village. There were no Israeli military posts in the village as on the Jordanian side and there were no political activists opposing the Israeli policy, therefore there was no harassment from the security system. On the other side, the presence of the Jordanian army was keenly felt. The Jordanian army had posts along the border and a checkpoint at the entrance of the village.

East Barta'ans on the other hand, did not undergo significant changes and were able to integrate into the West Bank, Jordan, and the Arab world. They continued to live in the same cultural, linguistic, and social environment. Their economic situation was difficult for the first years. Agriculture continued to be the main source of income for most of them. Work opportunities in both parts of the village were limited and residents were forced to seek work outside their villages. Some East Barta'ans had to travel to the Gulf States or to European countries to find work and send some of the money back to support their families. Many of them did not return.[21] However, there was no significant change in the living standard among those

---

20   They worked in groups in the nearby towns and cities. They lived in wretched conditions and went home only on weekends (Kabha 1986).

21   There are more than one thousand people originally from East Barta'a abroad.

who stayed behind. They maintained their lifestyle and consumption patterns (Amara and Kabha 1996).

As indicated earlier, Jordan did not invest in the infrastructure of the West Bank, but in the early 1960s there was a significant change in the village when it was decided to connect it to its nearby localities. East Barta'a and other border villages were considered important strategic sites to the Jordanians, unlike the Israelis who neglected their border villages. Jordan decided to connect Barta'a to Jenin. A bus company, "The Frontier Lines," ran regular transport and enabled the residents to integrate into the political, economic, and cultural fabric of the West Bank. Unlike their brothers across the border, their integration was smoother and easier.

After the division, East Barta'ans had to build two schools (one for boys and another for girls) that were considered modern compared to the wretched school in the western part. The bus line enabled students to continue their studies in the nearby towns.[22]

During the years of separation, the two communities developed several differences between them. The living standard of West Barta'ans was higher than on the eastern side. East Barta'ans, on the other hand, boasted a high percentage of university graduates and had personal mobility in political, social, and cultural spheres under Jordanian rule.

Palestinian Citizens of Israel and the Occupied Territories: 1967–1987

The Arab world expected to liberate the Palestinian homeland in 1967 war. Instead, it became a humiliating defeat. The remainder of the Palestinian people living in their homeland fell under Israel's occupation. The war was a blow to Pan Arabism but served as a take-off for Palestinian nationalism and resistance. Since then, the PLO emerged as the main Palestinian organization and gradually received broad international recognition.

As for the Palestinians in Israel, the war enabled them to reestablish family, cultural, and political ties with the Palestinians in the West Bank and

---

22 Only few continued their studies compared to the eastern part. Mar'i (1976) conducted research on the three divided villages (Barta'a, Baqa, and Beit Safafa) and found that academic graduates from the Jordanian side outnumbered those from the Israeli side as a result of different priorities between the two groups. Palestinians in the West Bank and the Diaspora invested in education as a means of personal and national mobilization. Palestinians in Israel were not properly qualified to continue their academic studies during their high school years. When joining Israeli universities, they experienced a cultural shock, while their brethren across the border did not face these difficulties.

Gaza Strip. Under PLO influence, they were redefined as an integral part of the Palestinian nation, and their self-respect and dignity were "rehabilitated" especially after the Land Day in 1976.[23]

Smooha (1991) claims the Palestinians in Israel became more politically involved, more critical of the state policy against them, and more insistent on equal rights and opportunities. They increasingly rejected their marginal status and sought greater integration in the Israeli society. In the 1970s, a new educated and articulate leadership replaced the old co-opted one. New forums emerged to deliberate all matters of Palestinian concern, claiming representation of the entire community, and fighting for official recognition.[24] The change in Palestinian voting patterns was also substantial.[25] They fought to attain the status of a national minority with an officially recognized leadership, control of their own institutions, and the right to form new ones.

They also fought to win legitimacy for their Palestinian nationalism by having their Palestinian identity, heritage, and culture accepted and their solidarity with the Palestinians and support for the PLO tolerated. They did not want to be treated as a subversive element. Their support for the PLO reflected their deep identification with the Palestinian cause and the endorsement of the idea of two states for two peoples, yet they did not want to be part of the emerging Palestinian state (Ghanem 1996). The state and the Jewish majority viewed this change as a hostile development and resented it.

Meanwhile, when Israel took control of the West Bank and Gaza Strip in 1967, it did not officially consider them "occupied," claiming they were not taken from a legal owner. Israel also claimed to have governed them according to the Geneva Conventions that governs conduct in occupied areas. The occupation was supposed to be temporary but a date has never been set for withdrawal. According to the Geneva Conventions, the occupier was not supposed to enact any changes in the territories that would prejudice their nature and future, yet Israel introduced numerous changes and committed gross violations of these conventions such as massive land confiscations, deportations, and house demolitions.

---

23 A general strike was announced for March 30, 1976, to protest land expropriations in Galilee. Clashes erupted, and six protesters were killed by the Israeli army. This was a landmark in the history of the Palestinian struggle in Israel.

24 Such as the Supreme Follow-Up Committee and the Committee of the Heads of Arab Local Councils.

25 The Jewish parties and their affiliated Arab lists won from 77 percent to 89 percent of the Palestinian vote during the 1949-65 Knesset elections, declining to 71 percent in 1969, and 49 percent in 1984. The traditional Arab lists failed to win any seats in 1981 and disappeared thereafter (Smooha 1991).

Israel imposed partial integration of the West Bank and Gaza Strip. Jordanian, Egyptian, and Israeli military laws administered the occupied territories. The road system, electricity grid, telephone network, and water supply were integrated into Israel. Over half the land was seized and the use of water resources was tightly restricted. A third of the labor force in the West Bank and 70 percent of Gaza Strip staffed the cheapest and most undesirable jobs in Israel.[26] The revenues collected from Palestinians and those working inside the Green Line were much higher than the economic costs of occupation. Over 100,000 Jews settled in the occupied territories and enjoyed cut-rate, quality housing and received enormous subsidies (Benvenisti 1989).[27]

Despite the discriminatory Israeli policies, Palestinians maintained separate institutions of their own. They expanded the network of voluntary associations and built eight colleges. Pro-PLO nationalist leaders replaced their pro-Jordanian traditional notables. They showed all forms of resistance, including violence, and in return Israel used repressive and collective punishment to contain them. They clearly drifted away from Pan Arabism and reasserted themselves as Palestinians (Smooha 1991). For most of the Palestinians, occupation meant a life of daily harassment, humiliation, and exploitation by soldiers at roadblocks and checkpoints, by officials of the military administration, by settlers, and by Jewish employers. Their common grievance was that they were not treated like human beings (Schiff and Ya'ari 1989).

"The Reunion" of Barta'a: 1967–1987

As far as the two parts of Barta'a are concerned, the most important consequence of the 1967 war was the dramatic reunion of the family. Nevertheless, both sides felt the reunion was half-hearted. The cultural differences that had developed during the years of separation were significant and caused a feeling of suspicion and alienation between them. Each side tended to reject the other. Only the older generation reactivated their contacts and recaptured mutual memories and experiences (Amara and Kabha 1996).

From the time the two parts renewed their contacts, there was a feeling of enmity and of superiority of each over the other.[28] The years of separation

---

26 In construction, agriculture, industry, and low-status service.

27 At that time, they constituted 3 percent of the population in the West Bank and Gaza Strip, and 2 percent of the population of Israel.

28 West Barta'ans considered themselves modern, competitive, and open-minded compared to their brethren in the eastern part, while East Barta'ans considered themselves more conservative, religious (in the positive sense), and educated. Their national consciousness was much more developed than those across the border.

and yearning turned into alienation and hostility. A set of mutual negative images existed between the two larger Palestinian communities (Palestinians in Israel and in the West Bank) based on superficial contacts between them (Kan'ana 1976).

The "reunion" did not unify the two parts of the village. The political status of the residents in both parts of the village remained different. The social differences that developed during the years of separation were strengthened by the political and administrative policies that were applied on them. Only West Barta'ans were Israeli citizens while East Barta'ans remained citizens of the Hashemite Kingdom and at the same time occupied subjects of Israel.[29] They received orange identity cards to distinguish them from the Israeli citizens with the blue identity cards.

The difference in their political status created administrative separation in all spheres. In addition, there was also voluntary agreement on their part to live separately. They continued to pray in their own mosques and to travel in separate buses to their workplaces. In time, West Barta'a, being part of Israel, was connected to the Israeli electricity grid, while East Barta'a was connected to the electricity grid financed by Jordan. The two communities continued to run separate educational systems with different curricula. They did not create common social frameworks. The road connecting the two parts of the village remained unpaved as East Barta'ans objected to its paving. They saw it as a symbolic act of "unifying the village and annexation to Israel." Only in the mid 1980s did both sides agree to join in some projects that served them both (Amara and Kabha, 1996).

Still both parts participated in some social activities, such as family festivities, mourning gatherings, and the football games held on Saturdays on the western side. During the first 20 years after the "reunion," there were only a dozen marriages between the sides.

As mentioned earlier, in 1966 the Israeli military administration was annulled and residents of West Barta'a integrated into the Israeli labor market. Most of them underwent professional training and others became private contractors. As a result there was a significant rise in the living standard of the village reflected mainly in their consumption patterns. Israel's occupation of the West Bank brought with it various changes in the conditions and lifestyles of East Barta'ans as well. By opening up work possibilities in Israel, some of them became economically dependent on the Israeli labor market. Since East Barta'a lies on the Green Line, its residents were even more

---

29 The territories were controlled according to the Jordanian civil laws and the Israeli military laws.

dependent on Israel than most West Bankers.[30] As a result, agriculture eventually turned into a marginal source of income in both parts of the village.

Even though both sides depended on the Israeli labor market, their status at work was different. West Barta'ans were protected and had better conditions, while East Barta'ans worked in humiliating conditions with no professional or social protection (as they were not allowed to join any trade union in Israel). By joining the Israeli labor market, East Barta'ans increased their per capita income considerably, but this did not change their consumption patterns and they continued to live modestly.

The economy of the occupied territories deteriorated considerably while the economic standard of the majority of the Palestinians in Israel significantly improved during that period. Until 1967, East Barta'ans enjoyed the benefits of infrastructure development more than West Barta'ans. The situation changed during the years of occupation. Israel did not maintain infrastructure of the West Bank in general and in East Barta'a in particular. As a result, all internal roads and the road connecting Barta'a to Jenin deteriorated. The schools in East Barta'a were left to deteriorate compared to the situation in West Barta'a where development was under way. All the internal roads in West Barta'a were well paved by this time. The differences between the two parts of the village became strongly visible and every visitor to the village could easily discern the dividing line between them.

The question to be raised in this context: Did the two Barta'as develop two different political orientations as the "divergence thesis" predicts or did they develop a similar political orientation as the "convergence thesis" predicts? As indicated earlier, the different political statuses of the two groups made them adopt different strategies. West Barta'ans, being Israeli citizens, chose the integration strategy, while the East Barta'ans adopted the survival strategy. The former emphasized their willingness to integrate into Israel, while the later emphasized their willingness to disconnect from Israel (al-Haj 1988). West Barta'ans learnt Hebrew, joined Jewish institutions, and accepted the existence of Israel in its 1948 borders. East Barta'ans, on the other hand, were linked to Israel only by military force and economic dependency. They learnt Hebrew only to get along with the Israeli authority and manage economically. They did not demand to be integrated into the Israeli political and legal system. Women with Israeli ID cards, for example, who married easterners gave up their Israeli citizenship.[31] Israeli citizenship

---

30 Ninety percent of the work force from East Barta'a worked in Israel compared to one-third of the labor force in the West Bank.

31 After the outbreak of the first *intifada* and the closure imposed on the West Bank they struggled to get their Israeli ID cards back and grant their spouses and children Israeli ID cards as well.

was not perceived then as an advantage to most East Barta'ans who preferred the Jordanian passport that gave them free access to the Arab world.

The only time the two parts united efforts was in August 1972 when they protested against the Israeli army bulldozers that tried to excavate a canal between a military training site and West Barta'a.[32] Men, women, and children from both parts of the village staged a sit-down and blocked the bulldozers. Although the act was initiated by easterners, it showed readiness on the westerners' part to protest against discriminatory Israeli policies. As a result, Moshe Dayan, then Israeli Defense Minister, agreed to reduce the size of the army's training area in the district.

Voting patterns are also an important indicator of West Barta'ans political behavior. They were active participants in every Knesset election. Their voting patterns have changed during the years; until 1967, Zionist parties got 90 percent of their votes but, later on, that gradually decreased.[33] Nevertheless, the overall trend remained the same as the village was dependent on the government's good will for any project in the village.

The reunion did not blur the border-line which continued to separate the two Barta'as. Bishara (1993) claims the 1967 reunion contributed to the polarization of the struggle conducted by the Palestinians in Israel who, being citizens of the state, demanded their democratic rights of equality. Although there was a certain process of Palestinization on part of the Palestinians in Israel, the basic differences between the two groups remained, especially vis-à-vis their collective identity. The struggle of Palestinians in Israel was evidence of their desire to integrate into the state, not to be separated. This was the beginning of a real "Israelization" process and their growing awareness of their civil rights. The process of democratization of the Israeli society during the 1970s enabled them to conduct a fierce democratic struggle.

On the other hand, East Barta'ans, like all Palestinians in the West Bank, experienced a transition from a Pan Arab minority to being the core of future Palestinian statehood, fighting for separation from Israel and building a state of their own (Smooha 1991).

---

32 The Israeli army seized 1000 dunams in 1967 for training purposes. The villagers used the stretch of land whenever the army was absent.

33 In 1977, the communist party got 51 percent of the overall Palestinian votes and 44 percent of Barta'a's (as a result of Land Day in 1976). In 1981, the Communist Party got 38 percent of the overall votes and 58 percent of Barta'a's. This was due to the residents' disappointment with the government's disapproval of the village map. In 1984, there was a drop for non-Zionist parties (17 percent), and the Labor party received the biggest chunk of votes (57 percent) due to the inauguration of the first Histadrut club in the village.

The First *Intifada*: 1987–1993

The first *intifada*, which erupted in December 1987, as a result of political, economic, and social pressures accumulated during the years of occupation, deepened the differences among the two communities. Palestinians in the occupied territories were the main players while Palestinians in Israel were only supporters and sympathizers. The former engaged in actions causing widespread disruption of daily life,[34] while the later showed approval as outsiders (Smooha 1991). The Israeli army responded by killing, wounding, and arresting thousands of Palestinians as well as imposing collective punishments (curfews, closures, house demolitions, and the disruption of basic services). Palestinians in Israel expressed their support by holding mass demonstrations, strikes, and donating money.

The first *intifada* had a paradoxical impact on the Palestinians in Israel. It reaffirmed their Israeli identity,[35] and at the same time deepened the Palestinization process that had started earlier. In the early 1990s, a consensus developed among the three segments of the Palestinian people: those under the occupation were supposed to continue with the *intifada*, those in the Diaspora were supposed to engage in international politics and diplomacy, and those within the Green Line were supposed to serve as a peace lobby within Israel.[36]

The first *intifada* symbolized the staunch readiness of the Palestinians under occupation to struggle despite the suffering and the sacrifice. They accepted all that in order to sever the ties and become politically independent. The first *intifada* led King Hussein to withdraw any claims to the West Bank by Jordan in August 1988. This, in turn, prepared the ground for the peace process with the PLO in 1993.

Barta'a, the First *Intifada*, the Gulf War, and the Suicide Bomb in Hadera: 1987–1995

The two Barta'as can be seen as a microcosm of the differences between the Palestinians in Israel and the Palestinians in the occupied territories. Located on the border, West Barta'a was affected more than any Palestinian locality in

---

34 They drew graffiti on walls, displayed Palestinians flags, stoned Israeli soldiers, boycotted Israeli products and taxes, held strikes, and shut down local commercial establishments at certain hours.

35 By accepting Israel and staying away from the intifada while playing a role corresponding to their status as Israeli citizens.

36 The PLO called on them to support any political party that would accept the principle of land for peace and an international conference as a framework for negotiation.

Israel. When East Barta'ans blocked roads, the army set a checkpoint at the entrance to West Barta'a. Most soldiers were not aware of the uniqueness of the village and many West Barta'ans fell victims between the army and the protesters from the eastern side.

The *intifada* weakened the mutual negative images and created a sense of solidarity and admiration between Palestinian communities. Nevertheless, it affected their social interaction and deepened the physical separation between them (Kabha 1990).

Although the western part was more developed than the eastern part, beyond that there was much underlying similarity.[37] The differences became more conspicuous during the *intifada*. Nearly all roads in East Barta'a were blocked to prevent the army from entering the village; Graffiti filled the walls and Palestinian flags hung on electricity poles. The *intifada* and the continuous strikes affected the economic situation of most of the population on the eastern side,[38] while the economic situation of the western side remained unaffected. The *intifada* also caused major changes in the social structure in the eastern part. The *mukhtar* and the older generation who ran the village resigned and the young generation who organized "popular committees" took over.

In 1991, the Gulf War sharpened the differences between the two parts. Only the western side got gas masks while the eastern side remained unprotected. Whenever an Iraqi missile fell on Israel, East Barta'ans got on the roofs and cheered while their brethren across the borders shut themselves up in sealed rooms. Although most interviewees from West Barta'a felt content that Israel was threatened, they all acted as Israeli citizens did (carried their gas masks wherever they went and shut themselves in sealed rooms).

The Gulf War and the closure imposed on the West Bank and Gaza Strip accentuated the economic deterioration of most Palestinians.[39] Since the closure was imposed, only a few East Barta'ans were given work permits in Israel, the rest were unemployed. Many of them had to return involuntarily to agriculture to survive.[40] Nevertheless, some infiltrated illegally to work in the nearby Arab localities in Israel.

---

37 In the early 1980s, the eastern part started building new houses as in the western part. Still the infrastructures of both parts were different (developed in the western part and neglected in the eastern part).

38 There was a drop of 50 percent in their income as a result of the continuous strikes and the 42-day-closure.

39 As a result of the weakening relationship with Jordan and the lack of aid from Gulf states.

40 The unemployment rate reached 90 percent in 1991, whereas West Barta'ans continued with their routine life.

In September 1993, the Declaration of Principles was signed in Washington between Israel and the PLO leadership, paving the way for the Oslo process. This was supposed to be a turning point for the Israeli as well as the Palestinian nation. Nevertheless, there were factions from both sides that disapproved of the new trend. In February 1994, a Jewish settler killed 29 Palestinians praying in a Hebron mosque, and two months later Hamas carried out three suicide attacks in Afula, Ashdod, and Hadera, killing 16 and wounding 76 Israelis. The suicide attacker in Hadera passed through Barta'a in a taxi from West Barta'a.[41] West Barta'ans condemned the act and complained against the negative media coverage of their village. A checkpoint was set up at the entrance to West Barta'a to check every passerby. West Barta'ans protested against it and recruited Knesset members in vain to have it removed (it was removed in June 1995). They saw it as a political act leading to their "annexation" to the West Bank.

Since the first *intifada*, and especially after the Gulf War, there has been a significant increase in marriages between the two sides of the village. At first, both sides were content with the new trend and looked at it positively as it weakened the alienation and enmity that existed between them. After the closure and the restriction on work permits, the mixed marriage phenomenon increased again, mainly among Israeli women moving to East Barta'a and acquiring Israeli ID cards for their spouses. The residents called the phenomenon the "ID card marriages" which was a unique strategy that East Barta'ans adopted to adjust to the restrictions imposed on them (Kabha 1992).

The economic dependence of East Barta'ans on the Israeli economy was an advantage for them prior to the *intifada* compared to other villages in the West Bank. The closure imposed on the West Bank after 1991, affected them deeply. For some, the only escape was getting an Israeli ID card by marrying a relative from the Israeli side. This was preferable to going through the bureaucratic procedures to get work permits. They saw in these marriages a way for improving their personal and economic status as it granted them professional protection, personal and economic mobility, and a permanent work place. Nevertheless, most East Barta'ans who had Israeli ID cards did not enjoy a much better economic status than those who did not, nor did they receive better treatment from the Israeli army during the first *intifada* (Kabha 1992).

We can ask whether kinship between the two parts and the continuous exposure of West Barta'ans to the first *intifada* brought them closer to the orientation of the East Barta'ans as the "convergence thesis" assumes,

---

41 Two residents from West Barta'a were arrested for two weeks and released with no charges.

or whether they maintained diverse orientations as the "divergence thesis" predicts. West Barta'ans, like the rest of the Palestinians in Israel, identified with their brothers across the borders.[42] Despite their complete solidarity, the *intifada* line was clear to them. Each side was interested in keeping the political status quo as it was, and in most cases they adhered to the rules of the game. West Barta'ans did not break the Israeli law. They supported their brethren morally and financially, and identified with their struggle without taking an active part in it.[43] Both sides understood that these activities were sufficient, and East Barta'ans were satisfied with the non-active participation of the West Barta'ans in the *intifada*.

West Barta'ans were active in their protest against the occupation but used acceptable democratic means.[44] The first *intifada* did not affect their voting patterns. In the 1988 elections, the non-Zionist parties received only 21 percent of the votes, despite the fact that the westerners were exposed to the suffering of their brethren in the eastern part. The fact that there was no local council in the village and no permanent government funding illustrates the total village dependence on the Israeli government.

During the *intifada*, both the Palestinian and the Israeli components in the identity of West Barta'ans were strengthened: "We have become more Palestinian without becoming less Israeli." Only a minority noted that the *intifada* influenced their position towards the state and the Jewish majority as a result of the army brutality against East Barta'ans. The positions expressed by this small group were not, however, converted into rebellious acts against their Israeli citizenship.

The support of the West Barta'ans for their relatives does not indicate any contradiction in their identities, claimed most interviewees. The only group of youngsters that was arrested from West Barta'a was accused of writing slogans, proclamations, and carrying Palestinian flags (November 1989). They were not accused of any attack, unlike many East Barta'ans who were active participants in routine *intifada* activities.

Israeli policy was different toward the two parts of the village depending on their political status: citizens and non-citizens. Although West Barta'ans frequently complained to the authorities about the unfair treatment of the army and the police toward them, they were always aware that they faced

---

42 They warned them when the army entered the village as they felt obliged to protect them. They donated money to build demolished houses and took part in strikes organized by the heads of the local Palestinian authorities in Israel.

43 They did not burn tires, block roads, hang flags, or stone army patrols.

44 They negotiated with government bodies and turned to the press in cases of offenses that were carried out against them.

a different attitude than that facing their brethren across the border. West Barta'ans did not suffer from curfews, house demolishment, they were not deported, killed or wounded, as were their brethren. East Barta'ans did not suffer any fatalities, but some of them were detained and several houses were demolished.[45] East Barta'ans were kept under military rule. The army could enter the village at all times for arbitrary searches and detentions. West Barta'ans did not get the same treatment. Only the police, not the army, was allowed to carry out a search with search warrants.

Barta'a: the Oslo Process, the Second *Intifada*, and the Apartheid Wall

Oslo II, signed in 1995, divided the West Bank to three zones: A, B, and C. East Barta'a came under the civil control of the Palestinian National Authority (PNA) as a part of the Jenin district.[46] East Barta'ans exchanged their orange ID cards given to them by Israel for the green Palestinian ID cards (with the same numbers) issued by the Palestinian Interior Ministry. Since then, the PNA became responsible for the education, health systems, and other social services while Israel remained responsible for security matters. West Barta'ans continued living as before.

In 1992, the Israeli Interior Ministry imposed a regional council on West Barta'a and six other villages, but in 1997 it was agreed to establish two elected regional councils in Wadi A'ra, one of which was the "Basma Regional Council" that included West Barta'a. In 2001, the first democratic elections were held, and 10 members were elected to serve the 3,000 residents of West Barta'a. Meanwhile, in 1998 a local council was set up in East Barta'a to serve its 4,000 residents. The local council received its budget from the PNA.

East Barta'ans were free to travel to cities in the West Bank (as well as to nearby Arab localities in Israel though it was formally illegal). Many of them still worked in Israel until the outbreak of the second *intifada* in 2000. Neither Barta'a took any active part in the second *intifada*, but since then, East Barta'ans faced restrictions on their movements as their village was a transit point to and from the West Bank. In 2001, it became quite impossible for people from East Barta'a to enter Israel, or even to cross the valley and visit their relatives in West Barta'a without being fined or arrested by the

---

45 12 houses were demolished and one house was sealed during the *intifada*.

46 The residential area of East Barta'a was considered zone B, the rest of the village was zone C; area C allowed for more Israeli presence than did B.

Border Police. Restrictions were especially severe during the construction of the Apartheid Wall. The army positioned tanks at the entrance of the village and harassed East Barta'ans who went in or out of the village.[47]

While East Barta'ans were increasingly hindered from working in Israel as further restrictions were imposed on them, they started developing their own market. Palestinians from Israel who were used to shop in Jenin found Barta'a's market an alternative. The market bloomed; more than 100 new stores and sewing workshops were opened.[48] Some of the owners were from Hebron, Jenin, and Nablus who rented houses in East Barta'a. The location of East Barta'a was an important strategic place as the only transit point to the West Bank. Each day more than 20 loaded trucks passed through the village bound for Jenin and Nablus. It was therefore in the interest of the PNA that East Barta'a should not take part in the second *intifada* and that the food convoys could pass through peacefully to the rest of the West Bank. The market in East Barta'a thus witnessed two prosperous years. Nearly 90 percent of its residents lived on trade.

Since the construction of the Wall in 2002, East Barta'ans suffered from being cut off from Jenin (their cultural, financial, educational, and health center) and from the rest of the West Bank. The Israeli military declared the areas west of the Wall a closed military area.[49] The consequences on village life were dreadful. East Barta'ans found themselves imprisoned in a cage and isolated from the outer world. People who wanted to get in or out of the village had to wait for hours to be checked.

In January 2003, the Israeli Authorities decided to demolish 72 houses and commercial shops in East Barta'a,[50] claiming they had been built without permits and were not in accordance with military orders.[51] The area threatened with demolition is the commercial heart of the village. The demolition would cause a real disaster for East Barta'ans and would kill its active commercial center.

---

47 People were prevented from going to Jenin, farmers could not attend to their land (in 2002 farmers could not pick their olives), and students were harassed on their way to their colleges.

48 There were 5 sewing workshops that employed 450 women, some from nearby villages. These women have become the main source of their families' income especially in villages that had 60 percent unemployment rate.

49 The Wall was built on 200 dunams of the village land. A closed military area means that owners cannot sell or rent their land without special permits from the Israeli military.

50 Including 12 homes, 56 commercial shops, 3 sewing workshops and a lamp factory.

51 The Israeli military distributed military orders stating that the owners should evacuate their houses and shops as a final warning before demolition.

In October 2003, the Israeli military rendered the area inaccessible to all, even those living there, unless they were granted permits from the Israeli "Civil Administration." This was after a suicide bomber passed through Barta'a's checkpoint on her way to the Maxim restaurant in Haifa. The people in East Barta'a refused to apply for permits to live in their own village, asserting that these Israeli measurements were aimed at Judaizing their village and annexing their property. The Israeli military response was an unbroken closure of the village for 15 days, which forced East Barta'ans to apply for the permits as it was the only option for even the remote opportunity to leave and reenter their village. However, the military continued to inflict harsh measures against them. The access gates along the wall were frequently closed or inconsistently opened for short periods of time.[52]

Teachers, university and college students, and workers were unable to reach their destinations in Jenin, and merchants from the West Bank were unable to gain access to their markets in East Barta'a.[53] There were some 150 women in East Barta'a who worked in the sewing factory, but with the closure of the village closure by the Wall they were not allowed to return to their homes in other parts of the West Bank. Some have been able to rent houses in the village, but the rest were forced to sleep in the factory.

Israel has made a ghetto of East Barta'a. East Barta'ans who travel in or out of their village face incredible difficulties when trying to bring in food and goods to their families. Israeli soldiers declared that food could not be brought in unless it is purchased and imported from "Israeli companies." This applied not only to larger shipments but to individuals as well.[54] The Wall made life a nightmare for many people.

The future of East Barta'a is still unclear. Many fear that Israel will annex it as it falls behind the Wall in the "seam zone." They know Israel is interested in annexing their land without adding more Palestinians to its population. The head of the local council of West Barta'a declared that he would like to reunite Barta'a and annex it to Israel but the head of East Barta'a's council rejected his suggestion. He claimed that East Barta'ans want to be free from the Israeli occupation and be part of a future Palestinian state even if it means separating the village again. The general impression from the interviews held was that most people in East Barta'a do not want to be disconnected from

---

52 At ten o'clock at night the gates were closed and nobody was allowed to move.

53 There are many teachers from the nearby towns who cannot get to school in Barta'a on time as soldiers delay them. There are 150 university and college students who study in cities in the West Bank and there are about 60 official employees who work outside Barta'a.

54 Products and goods coming into the village from the West Bank are turned back, forcing dependence on higher-priced Israeli goods.

the West Bank as they are part of its social, cultural, and political life.

East Barta'a has become divided within itself, between those who hold Israeli ID cards and those who do not (40 percent of East Barta'ans hold Israel ID cards). Residents with Israeli ID cards are able to cross the border and move freely in Israel, find work in the nearby Arab villages, get social and health benefits, and send their children to West Barta'a's schools. More than 300 children from East Barta'a go to school in the western part of the village. Only three residents have moved their residency to West Barta'a.

Getting an Israeli ID card was easier under the Labor government but became quite difficult under the Likud government.[55] The Israeli ID card does not guarantee its holder automatic Israeli citizenship. The Interior Ministry grants only residency not citizenship (applying for citizenship takes a very long time).

Collective Identity

How do Palestinians in Israel define themselves? The collective identity of a minority generally reflects its status within the society as well as its interaction with the dominant group. "Accommodating" minorities usually accept identities imposed on them, while militant minorities reject them and try to define new ones as part of their struggle to improve their status within the society (Smooha 1991). As indicated earlier, the process of crystallizing the Palestinian identity in Israel was slower and more complicated compared to other Palestinian groups as three different situations affected it—their relationship towards the state and its policy towards them as a minority; the development of the Israeli-Arab conflict especially the Israeli-Palestinian one; and the development of the Palestinian national movement as a distinct national entity in the 1960s.

Until 1967, the Israeli component was the dominant element in the identity of its Palestinian population. It was the result of an intentional policy initiated by Israel (which was partially successful due to the isolation of this community and its separation from the Arab world and the Palestinian nation). Pan Arabism was dominant at that time, therefore only a minority defined itself as Palestinian while the majority defined itself as "Israeli Arabs." After 1967, the Arab component was strengthened. Since 1973, and especially after the rise in the PLO's popularity in the international arena,

---

55 During the Labor Government in 1992-1996, anyone eligible who applied for an Israeli ID card got it within 3 months. During the Likud Government, Israel gave out temporary ID cards for one year that had to be renewed each year for three years until they got a permanent Israeli ID card.

Palestinians in Israel started to strengthen the Palestinian component of their identity (Nakhleh 1978). In the mid 1980s two thirds of them defined themselves as Israeli Palestinians (Smooha 1989).

Research on the collective identity of Palestinians in Israel started in the 1960s in the universities of Haifa and Tel Aviv. Both used the "conflict model" and assumed that Palestinians have two conflicting components in their identity: the Israeli and the national-Arab components. The model assumes that Palestinians in Israel live with ongoing internal psychological tensions and use different adapting mechanisms to balance between them (Peres & Yuval-Davis 1969).

Smooha conducted research with representative samples using the "accommodation model." He claimed that Palestinians underwent two parallel processes, not necessarily conflicting: "Israelization" (became bilingual and bicultural and tied their future with that of Israel) and "Palestinization" (full solidarity with the struggle of the Palestinians and their right to self-determination). He found that there was an increase in the accommodating identity among them. Rouhana (1993) criticized both models and presented an alternative model: the "accentuating model." He claimed that the Palestinian identity is the only internalized identity and that the Israeli civic identity exists only on the formal legal level. He differentiated between the three levels of identities: the formal-legal level,[56] the normative level,[57] and the identification level. He claimed that the Palestinian identity of Palestinians in Israel was accentuated as part of the Palestinization process that started in the 1960s. The Palestinian component became the only component in their national identity, due to the inner conflicts characterizing the structure they live in. Being excluded from the identity, symbols, and national goals of the state, they were forced to promote their Palestinian identity. The Knesset election reform law of 1985 further clarified the limitations of the Palestinians' capability to change their status within the democratic framework. Although Palestinians are Israeli citizens, Israel is defined as the state of the Jewish people and not the state of its citizens; therefore Palestinians are excluded from the priorities, goals, and ideology of the state.

This section examines the significance of "Israeliness" and "Palestinianness" of the West Barta'ans (which was accentuated according to Rouhana) and

---

56 They have been involved in the Israeli political and economic system through their active participation in the Knesset elections to improve their status and living standard within the state.

57 They have internalized some new social (mainly with regards to norms concerning gender relations and life styles), cultural, and political values as a result of the continuous interaction with Jewish society.

compares it to the "Palestinianness" of East Barta'ans who do not have a complex identity. In most research conducted on collective identity, interviewees were asked to choose one category out of a set of categories determined by researchers. This research was qualitative and based on in-depth interviews with open questions that had no defined categories. Each interviewee was asked to define his own national identity as well as the national identity of the group across the border.

The West Barta'ans belonged to three sub-groups: the first group (a small group) defined itself as Israeli Arabs without using the Palestinian dimension, the second (the largest group) defined itself as Israeli Palestinians, and the third (a small group) defined itself either as exclusively Palestinian or as exclusively Arab without using the Israeli component. All West Barta'ans defined East Barta'ans as being exclusively Palestinian.

All interviewees were asked the same questions based on the three different levels of identity: the formal-legal level, the normative and value level, and the identification level. The political and economic involvement of West Barta'ans was examined and it was purely Israeli,[58] while the East Barta'ans were not part of the Israeli political and social system. The interviewees from both Barta'as admitted that there were differences between them due to the Israeli citizenship that granted its beholders basic rights and various benefits that East Barta'ans did not have.

Interviewees from West Barta'a, even those who did not define themselves as Israelis, were Israelis at the formal-legal level. Being Israeli citizens, they were ready to abide by Israeli laws, saw themselves as part of the Israeli system and its political institutions, took an active part in the Knesset elections and turned to the Israeli authorities when they felt discrimination. As Israeli citizens, they received all their social services as well as their welfare benefits from Israel.[59] The Israeli currency was used in West Barta'a, not the Jordanian currency as in East Barta'a. There were economic differences between them as well. The work relations were one-way: all workers from West Barta'a worked in Israel (no one worked in the West Bank), while workers from East Barta'a worked in Israel and in the West Bank.

There were hardly any differences between the three sub-groups as far as the formal-legal level was concerned. Only few regarded the PLO as an additional representative beside the Israeli legislative authority. Interviewees

---

58 Demonstrated by their participation in the Knesset elections, their attitude towards bodies representing them and their village, their attitude towards the executive authority in Israel, their readiness to obey the Israeli laws, etc.

59 In West Barta'a projects were not financed by Jordan or the PLO as was the case in East Barta'a.

from East Barta'a, on the other hand, did not consider themselves Israeli; they were neither ready nor did they think it was their duty to obey Israeli laws. They defined themselves as Palestinians and considered the PLO their sole representative. They did not consider themselves as part of the Israeli political and welfare system, but they regarded their brothers across the border as part of the Israeli political system, and encouraged their struggle within it.

As for the second level concerning social and cultural issues, the aim was to highlight the differences between the two parts of the village without referring to the three sub-groups of West Barta'a. The interviewees were asked about the daily use of Hebrew, their reading habits of newspapers, watching television and listening to the radio, social and cultural differences, attitudes towards women's status in society, and other issues. There were significant differences in norms and values between the two groups. West Barta'ans had acquired the Hebrew language and had adopted part of Israeli culture while preserving their Arabic language and culture. They took more interest in events occurring in Israel and less in what happened in the Palestinian society and the Arab world.[60] Thus, they have become "quasi-Israeli" in the second level. East Barta'ans, on the other hand, remained culturally Arab Palestinians. They did not try to imitate the Jewish society. They were influenced by West Barta'ans in several spheres, such as wedding ceremonies and life style, yet the differences were still notable.

The interviewees from both Barta'as were conscious that the social and cultural differences between them partly stemmed from their different life experiences. Some even said there was a difference in their "mentality." The eastern part valued education as a tool that would help them build a future Palestinian state. The western part believed they were more open-minded and democratic compared to the other side, who were conservative and lived in a closed society. The more prominent differences appeared in spheres such as the status of women and the relationship between sexes.

The interviewees were asked about their position on unifying the village and its annexation. The majority of West Barta'ans preferred to stay in Israel, only few were ready be annexed to the Palestinian entity under certain terms.[61] The majority of the East Barta'ans preferred to belong to the Palestinian entity. The two groups were then asked what they would do if it were to be decided that the two parts be united and annexed to the opposite

---

60 They were less interested in the ministerial appointments or other internal affairs in the PNA.

61 It would have to be a democratic state in which all the rights would be protected as they are provided in Israel.

entity. The majority of West Barta'ans said they would oppose the decision vigorously even if it meant moving out. Does that indicate that they have become "Israeli" on the third level, the level of identification?

The interviewees from West Barta'a were then asked about their identification with the symbols of the state of Israel.[62] The majority expressed antipathy towards most of the issues raised and did not identify with the state at times of crises, such as the Gulf War and the first *intifada* (although there were a few who expressed the sentiment of belonging with most of the issues mentioned). The question arose—if most of them did not feel they were Israelis, were they then Palestinians? Did their "Palestinianism" have the same meaning as it did to East Barta'ans? They were asked about their identification with Palestinian symbols.[63] The majority did not consider Palestinian symbols appropriate to their situation as opposed to East Barta'ans who fully identified with them.

A close study of the data brings forth a divergence in the pattern of identification. It is based on the level of sentiment. The results can be classified into three distinct groups: the "assimilating group" which expressed identification with Israeli symbols and showed minimal identification with Palestinian symbols; the "adaptive group," the largest group, which expressed minimal identification with both worlds, the Israeli as well as the Palestinian; the "dissociating group" which expressed strong Palestinian identification and low Israeli identification.

The results indicate that the Palestinian identity was marginal among most interviewees from West Barta'a. This could be explained by their continuous isolation from the Palestinian nation and their need to integrate as marginal citizens in Israel. The exclusion of the Palestinians from the political and economic center is followed by their exclusion from the cultural center as well. Palestinians live in closed communities that belong neither to the Israeli world nor to the Palestinian world (Sulieman 1996). The state and all its apparatuses, mainly the education system and media, promote this kind of marginal culture.

The results show that we cannot see in the weakening of one component a corresponding strengthening of the alternative component, as most researchers have concluded. The two models that were presented earlier—the conflict and the accentuated models—assume that the two identities, the national-Palestinian and the civic-Israeli are positioned as a linear sequence

---

62 The flag, national holidays, the army, the police, the policy of Israel, and other symbols.

63 The flag, the national holidays, their readiness to participate in the building of the future state, being partners in Palestinian national aspirations.

and that they contradict one another. These researchers assumed from the start that there are only two ways to interpret and to understand the experience of Palestinians in Israel: either they are Israelis or Palestinians.

On the other hand, the "accommodating model" assumes that the two identities are situated on two parallel and individual levels. The groups that Smooha (1989) presents emphasize different combinations of identity features. The findings of this research present a similar picture. The group which had undergone assimilation emphasized their Israeliness, while the group of "segregationists" stressed their Palestinian identity. The only difference is that Smooha claims that the majority of the Palestinians have accommodating identities while the results of this research indicate that the major group, which defined itself as "adaptive" expressed reservations concerning both identities.

Bishara (1995) argues that Palestinians have been trying to find an alternative collective identity that reaches beyond the national level, by reviving and nourishing their ethnic and religious affiliation on the regional level and strengthening the status of the clan on the local level. These identities (communal, regional, religious, and the clan line) make up an alternative collective identity in place of the national identity, since they are convenient and solve many intrinsic contradictions.

The results of this research correlate with the results of the parallel research conducted by Amara and Kabha (1996) on identity and linguistic differences between the two Barta'as. The interviewees from both sides were asked to create a scale classifying identities according to their importance (Israeli, Arab, Palestinian, Islamic, and regional). Both researches found that the Islamic identity was the central identity, especially among West Barta'ans, as it was more convenient to deal with than the other identities.[64]

During this research, interviewees were asked about the Israeli citizenship as well. All interviewees from West Barta'a stated that there was inequality in the political[65] and civic rights[66] granted them compared to Jewish citizens. They also said there was discrimination as far as equal opportunities were concerned. Although there was some improvement over the years in most spheres, the gaps between Jews and Palestinians in Israel were still wide. The interviewees from both sides of the village felt Israeli citizenship granted

---

64 It had no specific demands like the other identities, and was easy to perform on daily basis.

65 The right to vote and to be elected, freedom of assembly, freedom of movement and speech, etc.

66 All the benefits that the state gives its citizens such as health services, social security, child allowances, government budget for local councils, etc.

Jewish citizens a national feeling of belonging beside a variety of civic rights. It enabled them full political and economic integration. They could identify with the state, its goals, and symbols. The significance of Israeli citizenship for the Palestinians in Israel was totally different. It granted them political protection and a variety of rights and benefits, though not equal to those given to the Jews, but did not give them a feeling of a national belonging. Although most of the interviewees expressed dissatisfaction with Israel's policies, no one among them was willing to join his relatives on the other side of the border, adopt their struggle, and sever his ties with Israel.

Conclusion

Until Barta'a was divided in 1949, it was a homogeneous village. Since then, belonging to separate political entities, the communities began to adapt to their new situations and soon developed their own distinct characteristics. While the occupation of the West Bank by Israel in 1967 made a renewal of family ties possible, it did not bring the two parts of the village closer together, but instead led to a sharpening of the differences that had developed during the years of separation. They continued to live side by side as distinct communities and developed political orientations that took their cue from the differences in their political status: citizens and non-citizens of Israel. It was this difference in their political status that was to reinforce the continued divergences.

Among the West Barta'ans, this renewed meeting, paradoxically, strengthened the "Israelization" process. It made them realize that as Israeli citizens, albeit second-class, they had an advantage over their brothers across the Green Line who were under occupation, in that their Israeli citizenship granted them a variety of political and civic rights denied to their brethren in the occupied territories.

East Barta'ans, like the rest of the Palestinians in the occupied territories, adopted a political orientation that advocated dissociation from Israel, thereby reinforcing their growing Palestinian nationhood. West Barta'ans, like the rest of the Palestinians in Israel, opted for equal civic and collective rights within Israel, without demanding territorial autonomy or independence. With time, the security surveillance over them was lowered and they began enjoying the fruits of the democratization process that enabled them to conduct a persistent, legal struggle for full equality. The first *intifada* deepened the differences between the communities. West Barta'ans extended moral and material support but took no active part in the actual struggle waged against Israel by their counterparts in the occupied territories.

The interviewees from East Barta'a defined themselves exclusively as Palestinians, whereas most interviewees from West Barta'a defined their identity in terms of Israeli and Palestinian components. That is, they defined themselves as Israeli on the legal-formal level, being part of the political and economic Israeli system which enabled them to lead their lives as citizens. They were "quasi-Israeli" on the second level where values and norms were concerned. Thus, in accepting certain Israeli cultural patterns, they differed from other Palestinian groups. At the same time, West Barta'ans expressed antipathy towards the symbols of the state of Israel. Since most of them felt they belonged neither to the Palestinian nor to the Israeli world, they had become a distinct group.

The interviewees from West Barta'a considered their Israeli citizenship important in that it granted them political protection and a variety of rights, but were aware that it did not guarantee them the same rights enjoyed by Israeli Jews.

When interviewing West Barta'ans, on nearly every subject they were asked, they compared themselves with their relatives on the other side of the border. Although Palestinians in Israel never openly advocated these kinds of comparisons, West Barta'ans always made this comparison during the research due to their proximity to their brothers across the border and the continuous interaction between them. They referred to the "half filled glass and the half empty glass" on nearly every subject, even though on many questions they were not asked to do so. They always mentioned their inferior status in comparison to the Jews, yet they always added that it was much better than the lot of their brothers on the other side of the border. Most of them saw the deprivation of Palestinians in Israel in a wider perspective. They compared their situation to that on the other side of the border and pointed out what happened in the course of time. They had no illusions about their present position being satisfactory, but when they compared it to that of the military rule in the past or with that of the Palestinians in the West Bank or in the Gaza Strip who were deprived of their basic human rights, they felt better off. West Barta'ans knew what it meant to be without Israeli citizenship. It meant that your basic freedoms and rights were not guaranteed (freedom of movement, assembly, and the right to work etc).

East Barta'ans with Israeli ID cards were aware that their Israeli ID cards did not guarantee them political protection like their brothers in West Barta'a, but at least it gave them some basic rights (freedom of movement and the right to work) and some social benefits. The Israeli ID cards did not change their collective identity; they continued defining themselves exclusively as Palestinian and refused to be defined as "Israeli Palestinians."

They were called Palestinians with Israeli ID cards. The large number of "ID marriages" reflected the deep despair and the social and political confusion among East Barta'ans.

The mutual, though unspoken, agreement and interest of both communities—the Israeli Palestinians and those from the West Bank and Gaza Strip—is to accept the deviations in their identities. Under these circumstances their orientations differ as well. Only the future can tell whether there will come a time when a real reunion between the communities, can occur and their orientations coincide, so that their identities may develop individually and collectively in whatever direction they may wish to choose. Meanwhile, their differences hold implications for a possible future return of Palestinian refugees.

Bibliography

Al-Haj, Majid (ed.). 1988. "The Cultural and Political Consequences of the Meeting between the Palestinians across the Green Line." In A. Sofer, ed., *Twenty Years to the Six-Day War*. Haifa: University of Haifa.

Amara, Muhammed and S. Kabha. 1996. *Split Identity*. Giva'at Haviva: The Institute of Peace Research (Hebrew).

Benvenisti, Meron. 1987. *Lexicon of Judea and Samaria*. Jerusalem: Kane (Hebrew).

———. 1989. *The Dance of Fear: The Intifada, the Gulf War and the Peace Process*. Jerusalem: Keter.

Bishara, Azmi. 1993. "The Question of the Palestinian Minority in Israel," *Theory and Criticism*, 3:7–20 (Hebrew).

———. 1995. "The Israeli Arab: Reading in a Disrupted Political Discourse," *Majjallat Al-Dirasat Al-Filastiniya*. 24:26–54 (Arabic).

Ghanem, Asaad. 1996. *The Political Participation of Arabs in Israel*. Haifa: University of Haifa (Ph.D dissertation, Hebrew).

Kabha, R. 1986. *Barta'a*. Giva'at Haviva: Institute of Arab Studies.

Kabha, S. 1990. "On the Village Border," *Ha'aretz*. January 11 (Hebrew).

Kabha, Z. 2003. *Barta'a—The Split Heart*. Published by the writer (Arabic).

Kan'ana, Sharif. 1976. *Channels of Communication and Mutual Images between the West Bank and Arabs in Israel*. Bir-Zeit: Bir-Zeit University (Mimeographed).

Lehman-Wiltzig, S. 1993. "Copying the Master? Patterns of Israeli Protest 1950–1994," *Asian and African Studies*, 27: 129–147.

Lustick, Ian. 1980. *Arabs in the Jewish State: Israel's Control of a National Minority*. Austin: University of Texas Press.

Mar'i, S. 1976. "High Education in Three Divided Villages between Israel and the West Bank," *Hamizrah Hahadash*, pp. 27–36.

Nakhleh, K. 1978. "Cultural determinants of Palestinian collective identity," *New Outlook*, 18:31–40.

Osaski-Lazar, S. 1990. *The Positions of Arabs in Israel Towards the State 1949–1967*. (M.A. Thesis). Haifa: University of Haifa.

Peres, Y. and N. Yuval-Davis, N. 1969. "Some Observations on the National Identity of the Israeli Arabs," *Human Relations*, 22: 219–223.

Rekhess, Elie. 1989. "The Arabs in Israel and the Arabs in the Territories: Political Affiliation and National Solidarity 1967–1987." In A. Leech, ed., *The New East, A Special Edition on Arabs between Religion and National Awakening*. Jerusalem: Magnes (Hebrew).

Rouhana, Nadim. 1990. "The *intifada* and the Palestinians of Israel: Resurrecting the Green Line," *Journal of Palestine Studies,* 19(3):58–75.

———. 1993. "Accentuated Identities in Protracted Conflicts: The Collective Identity of the Palestinian Citizens in Israel," *Asian and African Studies,* 27:97–128.

Rosenfeld, H. 1959. "Changes in the Occupational Structure of the Arab Village," *Mebifnim*, 6:63–71 (Hebrew).

Schiff, Ze'ev. and Ehud Ya'ari. 1989. *Intifada: The Palestinian Uprising: Israel's Third Front*. New York: Simon and Schuster.

Shlaim, Avi. 1988. *Collusion across the Jordan: King Abdullah, the Zionist Movement, and the Partition of Palestine*. New York: Columbia University Press.

Smooha, Samy. 1980. "Existing Policies and Alternatives Regarding Arabs in Israel," *Megamout*, pp. 6–37 (Hebrew).

———. 1988. "A Comparison between the Palestinians in the Territories and Israel as a Test for the Irreversible Annexation Thesis." In A. Sofer, ed., *Twenty Years After the Six-Day War*. Haifa: University of Haifa.

———. 1989. *Arabs and Jews in Israel*. Vol. 1. Boulder, CO: Westview Press.

———. 1990. "Minority Status in an Ethnic Democracy: The Status of the Arabs in Israel," *Ethnic and Racial Studies,* 13(3):389–413.

———. 1991. "The Divergent Fate of the Palestinians on Both Sides of the Green Line: The *Intifada* as a Test." A Paper Presented at a Conference: "The Arab Minority in Israel: Dilemmas of Political Orientation and Social Change." Tel-Aviv University. June 3–4.

Sulieman, R. 1996. *Self Categorization of Minorities: The Case Study of Palestinians in Israel*. Haifa: Department of Psychology, Haifa University (Hebrew).

Chapter 4

Crossing Borders, Retaining Boundaries

Kin-nections of Negev Bedouin in Gaza, the West Bank, and Jordan

Cédric Parizot

Introduction

In this chapter, I will analyze the cross-border exchanges that have been occurring over the last 50 years between the Bedouin in the Negev and their kin and network members who became refugees in the West Bank, Gaza, and Jordan after 1948. I examine how such encounters have linked cross border populations through an intricate web of relations, while still fostering feelings of difference, power relations, and thus reinforcing boundaries between these groups. In the sociology of return migration, this issue is extremely important for thinking and rethinking the meaning of the homeland and the relationship between the forced migrants and the population in the place of origin, even if that place is quite close, like our case.

The Bedouin in Israel are normally considered as separate and even isolated from their fellow Palestinians in the occupied territories. They are often dissociated from other Palestinians by evoking their supposedly widespread enrolment in the Israeli army or by referring to their unique cultural nomadic background, as opposed to that of sedentary Palestinians (Parizot 2001a:94–98). This image of uniqueness is encouraged by academic research. Scholars have traditionally approached the Bedouin within the limit of their legal and territorial inscription and within the framework of their binary relations with the State of Israel.[1] While many scholars have noticed cross border relations, this approach has tended to overlook their significance. Further, it has reinforced the idea of the Bedouin's isolation from their Palestinian neighbors. In this respect, research in the south of Israel and Palestine follows a similar pattern as that done in the north of the country, showing little interest in contacts across the Green Line (Tamari 1997). Even new research, such as that of Avram Bornstein (2002) on Palestinian workers crossing the Green Line in search of work in the central region of Israel, plays down the deep relationships that can emerge from such exchanges.

In the south, it is actually difficult to establish a sharp distinction between the Bedouin and their Palestinian neighbors. First, many Palestinian refugees are Bedouin, originally from the Negev.[2] Second, the Bedouin have engaged in regular exchanges with local populations in the West Bank, Gaza, and even in the Sinai and Jordan, as I discovered while carrying out my fieldwork in the Negev. These exchanges stretch the social, economic, and political spaces of the Negev Bedouin beyond the limit of their territorial and administrative statuses. It is difficult to dissociate them socially and culturally as a discrete society or culture from their Palestinian neighbors.

Nevertheless, it appears that cross border exchanges do not completely erase boundaries. While people continue to meet across borders, despite all the obstacles they encounter, they still nourish strong perceptions of difference and even social distance from each other. Many factors can explain these perceptions. It is not my aim to review them all in this article, but rather to evaluate whether cross-border encounters can foster such differentiation. Stressing the impact of border crossings should not lead to the extreme noted by Pablo Vila in contemporary borders studies. He explains that contemporary studies and theories about borders have been dominated by the "cross-border" metaphor so much that the idea that such encounters can also "reinforce" borders is totally overlooked (Vila 2003:317–22). As Ulf Hannerz (1997:545) reminds us, crossing borders often helps in reinforcing structures of power and inequality. We should thus analyze how such encounters can foster distrust, unease, and conflict, as well as new structures of power.

---

1   This is the case for anthropologists, such as Kressel (1975) or Jakubowska (1985); for more recent works, see Dinero (1997). Works by the geographer Avinoam Meir should also be cited (Meir 1996). On the issue of political ties between the Bedouin and the State, see Basson (1995) or Parizot (1999, 2001b).

2   Between 50,000 to 80,000 people fled or where expelled from the Negev between 1947 until 1951. Thus they amount to almost 10 percent of the number of estimated refugees between 1947 and 1949 (Morris 1997:297–98).

This research is based on field data I collected between 1996 and 2001 while I followed my hosts, in the North Eastern Negev, in an unrecognized village located 17 kilometers from Beersheba and 15 kilometers from the city of Dhahriyya (southern West Bank). It is thus mostly their experience that I give voice to here, even if I also try to express that of their Palestinian kin and networks.

In order to better understand the population we are dealing with, I will first present briefly the situation of the Bedouin in the Negev and what has fostered the idea of their unquestioned isolation. This idea is called into question by the extent of their cross border exchanges. Accordingly, in the second part of this argument, I evaluate the capacity of trans-border links to generate trans-border groups of solidarity and interests whose dynamics impact local processes at work among the population in their home environments. In the third part of this paper, I show that cross-border exchanges should not be analyzed from the sole perspective of their extent or their capacity to reunite scattered groups. Careful examination shows that they can also produce difference and distance, strengthening the power of existing State borders.

Isolation

The view of the Negev Bedouin as an isolated community finds its roots in the local discourses of actors. In recent history, the Bedouin have been through a process of differentiation and community building that they express in the public sphere.

Process of community building. During the first half of the 20th century, the Bedouin in the Negev, or as they used to call themselves, the '*arab al-saba*' (Arabs of Beersheba), were virtually sedentarized in the north of the Negev, living off agriculture and pastoralism. At that time, they maintained regular social and economic exchanges with the people living in the Sinai, in Gaza, and in the south Hebron mountains (Marx 1967; Kressel 1993). This situation changed radically during the 1948 war. From an estimated population of 60,000 to 95,000 in 1947, only 12,000 Bedouin remained in the Negev in 1951. The others found themselves in the West Bank, the Gaza strip, the Sinai, and Jordan where they subsequently settled. Included in different geopolitical spaces, each group underwent distinct social, economic, and political processes that fostered specific identities and political-economic interests.

The Bedouin who remained in the Negev underwent a process of spatial, social, and economic marginalization. Following the policies of forced resettlement and urbanization, they emerged as a semi-urban lumpenprole-tariat at the periphery of Beersheba (Parizot 2001a). Given a high rate natural growth, the descendents of the 12,000 Bedouin who remained in the Negev amounted in 2000 to 140,000 persons. Half of them inhabit seven planned towns exclusively reserved for them, and the other half resides in unrecog-nized villages along the main road axes of the valley of Beersheba. These localities are the poorest in the region and their populations rely on employ-ment in the Jewish cities in the Negev (Abu Rabia 2000; Marx 2000).

Alongside these upheavals, the Negev Bedouin have been involved in a process of ethnicization and community-building. At first this was fostered by the Israeli authorities who intended to dissociate them from the rest of the Palestinian Israelis. This was motivated by a divide and rule policy (Lustick 1980) and because the authorities wanted to be more efficient when dealing with a society already considered "unique." Thus they developed specific bod-ies and specific policies that created among the Bedouin a sense of common destiny. For instance, while the Bedouin hold the same status as Israeli Muslims, they were progressively distinguished from them. The category of "Bedouin" appeared fairly rapidly on official forms, next to Muslims, Druze, Christians, and Circassians. Herein lies the strength of the categorizations imposed by the Israeli legal system. Reiterated in formal and informal discourse and on administrative forms, these categorizations ended up shaping discourses and representations of Jews and Arabs in the country (Parizot 2001a).

The process of community-building was also enhanced by the Bedouin themselves. Like all category ascriptions (Barth 1995), it took place through a dialectical process in which they played a primary role. The reality of Otherness created by the drastic upheavals that affected this group facilitated the process of reconstruction of tradition, a process that took place within the framework of terms imposed by the dominant discourse and was often enriched by scholarly and folkloristic works. Since the 1950s, the Bedouin became the objects of much academic research by anthropologists, sociolo-gists, and political scientists. These works legitimate their portrayal as a dis-tinct society separated from their kin at the periphery of the Negev. Even if such scholars noticed the existing links across borders they never analyzed them in any depth. More significantly, a body of folkloristic research written in Hebrew by local administrators and sometimes the Bedouin themselves, came to be taken as written history by the Bedouin.[3] They found in these

---

3   See among others, the works of Sasson Bar-Zvi (1991), Faraj Sliman al-Hamamde (1996) or
    the book published by Moshe Shohat and Yosif Ben David (2000) earmarked for Jewish and
    Arab schoolchildren in Israel.

works the keys and the yardsticks to reconstruct the lost "traditions" of their "unique society." As a result, in numerous contexts, the Bedouin no longer use the ethnic label '*arab* (literally, Arab) to describe themselves, and which contrasted with the term *fellahin* to designate the neighboring Arab populations, as was still the case in the 1950s. Today they use the term *bedu*.

The internalization of this ethnic label has been strengthened by its recurrent manipulation in the political discourse of Bedouin leaders. In late 1970s, an "Association for the Defense of Bedouin Rights" was founded. In early 1980s, few groups were daring enough to formulate their demands as "Arabs" or "Palestinians," fearing that this would draw criticism from the authorities. As Jakubowska (1992) shows, the local actors preferred to express their demands as "Negev Bedouin citizens" to dissociate their claims and their conflicts with the State from the Israeli-Palestinian conflict. It was only after 1993, when the implementation of the Oslo agreement began, that the Negev Bedouin started also to formulate their demands as "Palestinians" (Parizot 2001b:135–143). This change happened at a time when the use of national Palestinian symbols had become tolerated by the authorities and when the Oslo agreements (1993) sanctioned a separation of the fates of Palestinians in the West Bank and Gaza and those with Israeli citizenship. At the end of the 1990s, when local leaders and members of non-governmental bodies expressed their demands as "Palestinians," they meant "Palestinian citizens of Israel." They stressed their need to be recognized as a national minority inside Israel. Still, in the Negev, many people still use the terms "Negev Arabs" or "Negev Bedouin," that highlights both the priority given by the Bedouin to the defense of the interests of their own community and the territorialization of their identity.

Gaza, Beersheba, al-Dhahriyya, and Jordan. The Bedouin, while separated from their kin and network by borders, nevertheless maintained contacts with them. In part they were assisted by the fact that these borders were not always stable or recognized; In the last 50 years, the borders of the State of Israel have been constantly reshaped.

In 1949, the Rhodes Treaty fixed the Armistice Line, also called the Green Line, as the de facto international border of Israel. The Bedouin who remained in the Negev often illegally crossed the new borders to visit their kin and neighbors in territories under Egyptian or Jordanian rule (Burns 1962). Others engaged in the smuggling of livestock and other goods from Jordan, Iraq, Saudi Arabia, and Yemen (Abu Rabia 1994) with the informal consent of Israeli officials (Parizot 2001a). It is difficult to evaluate the extent and the intensity of these flows of goods and people as there is little available data. According to Emanuel Marx (1974:20–21) these exchanges were quite intense. Today, some people in the region of Tel 'Arad argue that during that period, their families used to maintain close and regular contacts with the people of the Palestinian West Bank villages of Sammu' and Yatta'. All in all, these exchanges, together with the hospitality offered to infiltrators, allowed an important flow of information to occur within separated families and networks.

After the 1967 war, the Green Line stopped being an obstacle to movement. While it was maintained as a political border, the Israeli authorities allowed people to cross from both sides. According to the Allon plan, the political border was to remain the Green Line while the security border was to be extended all the way to the Jordan River. Moshe Dayan encouraged the flow of people and goods between Israel proper and the occupied territories (Bornstein 2002). This policy led to the linkage of Israeli electricity, water, and road networks with those of the newly conquered lands. Moreover, while Israel chose not to annex the West Bank, the Gaza Strip, and Sinai, it tightened its hold on them by launching a settlement policy that allowed the development of important centers of Israeli Jewish population beyond the Green Line. Thus, from being a de facto international border, the Green Line progressively became a statutory border (Yiftachel 1999). On the one hand, Jews were able to enjoy full political and citizen rights on both sides of the border, while Palestinians conquered in 1967 were refused citizenship.

In this new context, the Bedouin were able to further develop and strengthen links with their kin and Palestinian networks. People went shopping on a daily basis in the markets of Gaza and the South Hebron Mountains. Palestinians, in turn, became more and more dependant on the Israeli labor market. By the 1980s, 30 percent of their labor force was engaged in Israel (Farsakh 2005). Among Palestinians in the south, many were employed by the Bedouin in the construction industry, as shepherds, or as salesmen in Israeli markets. In the same period, the Bedouin also developed matrimonial alliances with members of their families from whom they had been separated in 1948. Later, they even sought their brides among peasant families. Moreover, the low dowry asked by Palestinians offered men the possibility to marry more than one wife (Lewando-Hundt 1978). These exchanges developed until the end of the 1980s.

The outbreak of the first *intifada* (December 1987) and later the Oslo process (1994) introduced dramatic changes. The Bedouin and the Palestinians encountered more difficulties in maintaining such exchanges as Israel imposed increasing security measures (Bornstein 2002). In fact, after 1994, while the Israeli army withdrew progressively from the main urban and rural zones designated as areas A and B, it tightened its control over these newly created enclaves, leading to a "Bantustanization" of the occupied territories (Legrain 1997:85–90; Farsakh 2002:14–15). These rearrangements rendered movement more difficult between the new enclaves inside the occupied territories, as well as between the occupied territories and Israel proper. Gazans could not anymore move out of the newly fenced-in Strip without obtaining a permit from the Israeli authorities at the Erez checkpoint. Although West Bankers could move without a permit by avoiding Israeli checkpoints and taking bypass dirt roads, they risked being caught. Conversely, it became harder for the Bedouin to enter Gaza. Consequently, people started visiting the West Bank more often where they could more easily avoid checkpoints, even during time of closures. Moreover, people invested more effort into visiting kin and relations in the newly accessible Jordan whose border opened as early as 1993, following the signature of the peace agreement between Jordan and Israel. While the readjustments following the Oslo period did not sever the exchanges between the Bedouin and their kin and networks in the occupied territories, they did reorient both their direction and intensity.

The situation worsened after the outburst of the second *intifada*. Israel raised more obstacles to movement, among them the requirement for Israeli citizens to have a permit to enter Palestinian areas. Additionally, on July 31, 2003, the Knesset passed the Nationality and Entry into Israel Law (Temporary Order), which prevents Palestinian spouses of Israeli citizens from getting a right to Israeli residency (UN Rights Committee 2003).[4] These new measures did not sever the cross-border exchanges, but they reduced them considerably and, more importantly, they defined them once more as illegal.

In brief, over 50 years, the different modes of administration imposed on the Bedouin by the Israeli authorities have contributed to the marginalization of this group as compared with their Jewish and Arab neighbors in the region. This marginalization has fuelled a process of sharpening ethnicity and the emergence of a feeling of community that is expressed in public and political areas. Of course, these processes are not over, and they do not account for the complexity of the situation of the Bedouin. They are constantly being challenged by practices across borders that the local actors continue to conduct out of the public sphere, in the non-event. These practices broaden their social, economic, and political spaces of relations beyond such perceived boundaries.

---

4   In November 2003, the constitutionality of this law was contested by local NGOs who petitioned the Supreme Court. For more details on this law, see www.adalah.org/eng/famunif.php, accessed on July 9, 2007.

Border Crossing and Deterritorialization

I would like to illustrate this tendency through the case study of the lineage of the Rashayde (sing. Abu Rashid). I lived among them between January and July 1996, January 1998, and July 1999, and I visited the village regularly until summer 2003. The cross-border practices of this group show to what extent such exchanges can widen the scope of relations of people and foster the emergence of trans-border groups of solidarity and interests.

Trans-border kinship groups. Before 1948, this *'a'ila* (lineage)[5] was relatively important and prestigious to the extent that its leader was the *sheikh* of a *'ashira* (tribe) named after his own lineage. The *'ashira* of the Rashayde was divided into two settlements: the first was located north-east of Gaza City where they cultivated their lands, and the second lived a few kilometers south of the town of Rahat on different land. In winter 1948, the Israeli army launched the Yoav operation to conquer the Negev (Morris 1997:220). The Rashayde, settled west of Beersheba, were expelled to the Gaza Strip, together with the other lineages attached to their *'ashira*. The second group, located north of Beersheba, was scattered. Some of its members fled to Jordanian territory to settle in the region of Dhahriyya or close to the capital Amman. A minority stayed in Israel where they were relocated, like many other groups, east of Beersheba on the land of other exiled tribes. This region was designated as an enclosed area (*muntagat al-siyaj* [Arabic]/*ezor ha sayig* [Hebrew]) and put under military administration until 1966 (Marx 1967).

While only two brothers stayed in Israel, 'Awad and 'Awude, they managed to maintain their former social status. 'Awad, the youngest, became the *sheikh* of the newly reconstituted tribe (Figure 2). It included groups of the pre-1948 *'ashira* that claimed a common descent with the Abu Rashid through a patrilineal ancestor and others allied to them through matrimonial exchanges. Other groups were of noble Bedouin lineage or clients who were the remaining parts of displaced tribes outside the border of Israel. They needed to be affiliated to a tribe in order to stay in Israel and to obtain Israeli citizenship. Thus, 'Awad and 'Awude fell into a similar situation to other members of displaced people of noble Bedouin lineages. Separated from their agnates after the conflict, they kept their status despite being in a minority in the newly recomposed *'ashira*. The young *sheikh* was ruling

---

5   The term I often translate as "lineage," refers to a group of people claiming a common patrilineal descent whose members hold themselves mutually responsible for any action susceptible to affect the symbolic capital of the group. Actually, a *'a'ila* is rather a group of cognates than a group of agnates (Parizot 2001b:51–53).

other former clients of non-noble lineages whose number was greater than that of the noble groups.[6]

After 1967, the opening of the Green Line offered an opportunity for the two brothers to renew strong ties with members of their family from whom they had been separated in 1948 and eventually to reconstitute the powerful lineage as it had been before 1948. These new relations were sanctioned by matrimonial exchanges between 1967 and the end of the 1970s. The first marriage took place as early as spring 1968. It was followed by four others which joined female Rashayde refugees in Gaza with sons of both 'Awad and 'Awude (Figure 2). During this period, these alliances constituted almost half of the marriages of the Rashayde, and more than 90 percent of the weddings inside the group. In the 1980s, the number of such matrimonial exchanges between Israel and the occupied territories remained stable with six weddings between the Rashayde living in Gaza (three women and one man), and al-Dhahriyya (two girls), though the proportion compared to the total number of marriages started to dwindle, as these alliances repre-sented less than a third of the total number of marriages (6/20). As a result, in the 1990s, these matrimonial exchanges created a very intricate network stretching between Beersheba, Gaza, and the West Bank.

Relations between kin remained rather dynamic in this period, despite the continuous rearrangements of borders and the stronger limitations of movements that were imposed during the Oslo period. At the end of the 1990s, I was living at 'Iyad's house, the son of 'Awad who had died in the early 1980s. I would go to Gaza with 'Iyad and his wife to visit his mother-in-law and brothers-in-law. As an elder among the Rashayde, he often took part in the economic or social affairs of his cousins. But, while 'Iyad used to pay them regular visits in the 1980s, the difficulty in passing the Erez check-point prevented him from keeping up the same pace of visits in the 1990s. Hence, he and his wife began to limit their visits to holidays and important events. In Hura, his agnates also married to Gazan women from their lin-eage would follow a similar pattern. The outbreak of the second *intifada*, in September 2000, further reduced such exchanges. 'Iyad and his wife, Am 'Awad, would seldom go to the Gaza Strip. They preferred bringing Am 'Awad's mother and sisters to Hura. Thanks to his connections in the Israeli administration, 'Iyad easily obtained permits for them.

In the 1990s, the cross-border exchanges of the Israeli Rashayde were more intense with their agnates in the south of the West Bank and had just

---

6   For details concerning the restructuring of the tribal system under the Israeli administration, cf. Parizot 2001a: 45–52.

begun to develop with Jordanian kin. While it was easy for the Israeli army to control the newly fenced-in Gaza Strip, it was rather more difficult to do the same in the large open areas of the Southern Hebron Mountains. Like many neighboring groups in the Negev, most of the Rashayde would shop in the local market of al-Dhahriyya (West Bank). Throughout the 1990s, this little town of less than 30,000 people saw its market grow beyond the needs of its hinterland and become a center of exchanges. The market offered an extreme diversity of services and goods adapted to the demands of the Bedouin customers: from car repair to jewelry shops, from hairdresser studios for brides to shops for building materials and housing needs, and so on. The stolen-car and car-part markets also developed according to the demands of the Bedouin, influencing in turn the choice of cars targeted by thieves inside Israel. During this period, the region of al-Dhahriyya also became a center for labor recruitment. Palestinians went there in search of jobs inside Israel and more specifically with the Bedouin who would hire them with or without permits, mainly in the building industry.[7]

By the mid-1990s, the region had become such a center for exchange that young Bedouin invested in creating a well-organized system of taxis and minibuses between Dhahriyya and the Beersheba area. The youth of neighboring groups of the Rashayde living in the region of Hura took an active part in this transportation network.

'Iyad and the member of his family would pay frequent and spontaneous visits to their agnates in the town of Dhahriyya. The sons of Hamdan had a few houses there. Some of the Israeli Rashayde even had residences in the town. One of 'Iyad's brothers, Hisham, who was married to one of Muthgal's sisters, often went to meet his second wife and her children who chose to settle close to her brother in al-Dhahriyya. He thus resided between his three wives in Beersheba, Hura, and al-Dhahriyya.

Such visits could also include moments of leisure. 'Iyad would work in Beersheba as a car salesman. After a meeting he would come to have a lunch with his patrilineal cousin Muthgal, before going back to Beersheba for a second meeting. One evening in summer 1998, while we were watching France play Saudi Arabia in the Football World Cup, Muthgal phoned a few

---

7   At the beginning of the 1990s the number of Bedouin building firms increased parallel to the growing demand in construction following the massive arrival of Russian immigrants. At the end of the 1990s Bedouin employers increased as the Bedouin were promised by Ehud Barak, who was running for prime minister in the 1999 elections, that building demolitions would cease in the unrecognized villages. Consequently, people who used to live in light constructions began to build concrete structures. White blockhouses thus started to appear outside of planned towns.

times, teasing us that the Saudis would defeat the French. 'Iyad decided to watch the rest of the match at his cousin's house, as he found this interaction exciting. We waited until half time and went to see the second half of the match in al-Dhahriyya.

Throughout this period, 'Iyad also went to Jordan five to six times a year, in order to attend the main events in the life of his Jordanian family, such as marriages or holidays, as well as to take vacations. The Rashayde from Jordan used to pay regular visits to their agnates in Israel. Jaffal, the eldest son of Hamdan, living in Zarqa, close to Amman, often came to Israel for periods of one to three weeks. He was a central figure in the Jordanian branch of the lineage. His visits would be celebrated by successive dinners among his cousins (*awlad 'am*) in the village of the Rashayde, and he used to take an active part in local family affairs. He was invited to meetings of the local elders when crucial decisions had to be made, and he intervened many times in arbitration between local rivals of the Israeli branch. Between 1998 and 2001, 'Abd al-Karim, Jaffal's brother from Zarqa, also came regularly, but for longer periods of time, from two to six months. He entered Israel to work in menial jobs that provided him with a better income than his official work in Jordan as a teacher of mathematics. His son, Samir, came for an even longer period of time. He stayed in the 'Arab al-Rashayde for a year and a half between 1998 and 1999, and subsequently settled there in 2001. He worked in an Israeli food factory, learned Hebrew and even got engaged for a short while to a girl from a neighboring lineage of the Rashayde in the town of Hura. This failed engagement was originally intended for him to obtain Israeli citizenship. Women also came to Israel: Jaffal's and 'Abd al-Karim's wives visited a few times. These reciprocal visits helped strengthen family ties. Already, in 1996, one of Jaffal's daughters got married to 'Awude's youngest son. Later, in summer 2003, 'Ayayde, one of 'Iyad's brothers, married his son to another of Jaffal's daughters.

After the second Intifada started, while the exchanges with the Dhahriyyan Rashayde became more sporadic, those with the Jordanians went on at the same pace, and their presence in Hura became almost permanent, with only short periods of absence.

Trans-border configurations of power. At the end of the 1990s, these networks were all the more dynamic as members of the lineage used their connections with each other to enhance their own social status. For instance, 'Iyad and his cousin Muthgal, the eldest son of Hamdan living in al-Dhahriyya, developed their reciprocal ties in order to reassert their position against their rivals among the Rashayde as well as to readjust their respective positions in their local surroundings. Muthgal was older than 'Iyad. Enrolled in the Fateh movement since the 1970s, in the 1990s he obtained a respectable position as an official when the Palestinian National Authority was created. Working in Hebron, he was in daily contact with high-ranking Palestinian officers. This allowed him to position himself as a useful intermediary. He displayed this potential to his cousin 'Iyad as well as to his other Israeli agnates.

Strong efforts were exerted by these members of the Rashayde to construct a wide network of connections. Between January and March 1998, Muthgal invited his cousins almost twice a month to generous lunches or dinners, to which he invited high-ranking officers of the Palestinian security services or local and regional figures. 'Iyad was keener on building connections with such Palestinian personalities than his other Israeli kin, so he attended these gatherings regularly. Through repeated meetings he engaged in close and sometimes intimate relations with some members of the establishment of the region of al-Dhahiriyya. At the end of 1998, he even invited these Palestinian officers to family events in Hura. His contacts became so close that he sometimes took them on trips inside the Green Line, spending leisure time together as far as Tel-Aviv.

Within two years, 'Iyad and his patrilineal cousin built an important and effective network, which significantly improved their respective positions on the local and regional levels. 'Iyad managed to position himself as an indispensable intermediary for some of his neighbors and family members, especially those who often paid visits to the West Bank, as he could provide them with protection. One day, in the spring of 1999, he was asked by one of his acquaintances, an elder from a lineage in Ksifa, to help him free his brother from jail in Hebron after he was arrested by the Palestinian police. A few hours later, 'Iyad made a phone call to an officer in the Palestinian police in Hebron. The man was freed. 'Iyad also started to play the role of intermediary with higher figures in the Negev who would search for privileged contacts with Palestinian officials.

Such trans-border networking strategies became a common trend in the Negev at the end of the Oslo period. Ambitious Bedouin personalities intended to raise their power from the local to the regional level by cultivating such relations with the Palestinian Authority. Throughout this period, Bedouin notables sent symbolic funding to the PNA, they went on personal visits to Yasser Arafat, or organized delegations for the celebrations of the 'Eid al-Adha. This attitude was driven both by ambition and by a need for acknowledgment. In this sense, the trend corresponds to that of other Israeli Arabs who sent delegations to the newly opened countries of the Arab world such as to Jordan, as a way to compensate for a long-standing marginality (Rekhess 1996). 'Iyad took part in many such delegations. At this period, some Bedouin even planned to send a delegation with Talab al-Sana', a member of the Israeli Parliament, to visit President Saddam Hussein in Iraq.

Such cross-border or international networks were often exhibited to clients. In November 1998, during the municipal election in the Negev Bedouin town of Rahat, the candidates for the municipality disseminated brochures showing their pictures in company of Israeli officials as well as with Yasser Arafat. They intended to persuade their voters they could still count on them while visiting the Palestinian territories. An acquaintance of 'Iyad even tried to smuggle in a high-ranking officer of the Palestinian Intelligence Services in order to bring him to a meeting of one of the candidates in Rahat, but the officer was stopped by the Israeli police and sent back to al-Dhahriyya.

In short, cross-border relations of the Rashayde pertain to a general trend in the Negev which gave rise to cross-border groups of solidarity and interest, in other words, to trans-border configurations of power. This trend impacted on local social, economic, and political processes at work among the Bedouin as well as among their Palestinian neighbors. Likewise, social, economic, and political ties ensured a flow of goods, people, and values that eventually fostered the dissemination of cultural practices and representations. It is not my aim to elaborate on this last point, but many examples can be drawn from the literature on the Bedouin. The dissemination of practices and representations was noticed as early the 1970s on modes of celebrations of marriages (Lewando-Hundt 1978), religious beliefs (Jakubowska 1985), genealogical techniques (Parizot 2001a:80–81), or models of authorities (Parizot 2001a:135–43). In sum, cross-border relations extended the social, economic, and political spaces of the Bedouin and their Palestinian neighbors along a line stretching from Gaza, Beersheba, al-Dhahriyya, and Jordan.

An Unequal Frame of Relations

Nonetheless, it is insufficient to understand these cross-border exchanges only from the point of view of their capacity to extend networks of connections, or their context as a sharing of culture. These exchanges are taking place in a highly unstable political and spatial context, where borders are constantly redrawn and the statuses of people are redefined in ways that have often broadened the gap between cross-border "partners." Thus, while cross-border relations bring people closer, they also appear to be channels where differences are experienced and reconstructed, sometimes leading to conflict. Such processes take place even among trans-border kin and even while people are maintaining close and intimate relations.

Growing inequalities. Before the beginning of the first *intifada* (December 1987), the Bedouin and their fellow Palestinians already experienced their inequalities on a few levels, such as their distinct legal status and standards of living. At the beginning of the 1990s, these differences became sharper. The creation of the Palestinian National Authority did not lead to an improvement in the situation of Palestinian citizens. On the contrary, the tightening control by Israel over the new Palestinian areas, its new system of permits, and its closure policy considerably reduced their capacity of movement in comparison to that of their Bedouin kin and networks. The unfolding of the Oslo process revealed the weak and limited power of the PNA compared to Israel. In the end, the new regime did not give more freedom of expression or social advantages to the Palestinian citizens. Kin and others in the network of the Rashayde would often complain to their Israeli kin of their situation and of their discontent with the obvious corruption inside the PNA, the injustice, and the lack of freedom of expression. In this context, the Bedouin had no reason to envy them. While they would themselves often complain about the discrimination inside Israel, they still felt better off than their relatives.

Furthermore, this new context created new dependencies of the Palestinians upon their Bedouin Israeli networks. On the one hand, procedures to obtain work or visit permits required the mediation of an Israeli citizen who had to apply to the authorities on behalf of his Palestinian acquaintance. The Israeli intermediary would need to invest a lot of effort as well as a significant amount of his time in order to succeed with the complicated bureaucratic apparatus. On the other hand, Palestinians who were ready to take the risk of entering Israel illegally would also be dependent on the good will of their Israeli Bedouin counterparts, whether to find a way of transportation or to find a place to hide once inside the Green Line. Such exchanges potentially compromised Bedouin who could be discovered by the authorities. In brief, whether on legal or illegal grounds, the invitation of kin and network, which used to be a benevolent act before the 1990s, began to appear as a favor. After the eruption of the second *intifada*, the situation worsened because every illegal entry into Israel was punished more harshly by the Israeli authorities. While before the second *intifada*, Israel had rarely prevented illegal entries in the south of the West Bank, after 2000, the army tightened its control and made it more difficult to cross the Green Line. The Bedouin would thus have to take greater risks while helping their Palestinian kin or networks. During the 1990s my host expressed his anxieties. Even before the start of the second *intifada*, 'Iyad complained many times that his cousin Muthgal regularly asked him to come to al-Dhahriyya to pick him and high-ranking officers of the Palestinian Authority up in order to enter Israel illegally and visit local personalities. While 'Iyad was indeed benefiting from his participation in these visits, he was still frightened of being caught with his guests by the Israeli army or police.

On the economic level, the gap between the Bedouin and their Palestinian kin and network also widened tremendously as the Palestinian economy entered a crisis during the Oslo period (Arnon et al. 1997). The feeling of inequality increased as the Palestinians became more dependent on the dwindling work opportunities in Israel. Moreover, providers of services and market traders inside the West Bank more than ever needed the Bedouin to come to the occupied territories to purchase the cheap goods and services they were offering. The domestic Palestinian market could not ensure the same level of prosperity for their businesses. Among the Rashayde, people were asked for loans by their kin and networks on the other side of the Green Line. This gave some the opportunity to get a stronger hold on their kin's economic affairs. It is through such help that 'Iyad ar-Rashayde managed to become the owner of a building in the refugee camp of al-Breij (Gaza Strip). In the mid-1980s, the husband of his wife's sister, Ahmed, had borrowed a large sum of money in order to construct his four-story house. As the economic situation worsened, Ahmed could not reimburse the sum he borrowed from 'Iyad. As a consequence, he made him the owner of half of the building.

Since 1993, the date of the opening of the Jordanian border, 'Iyad and his Israeli kin were also able to measure the gap separating them from their Jordanian kin. While Jaffal, Hamdan's eldest son was a well-off businessman; his brothers and other cousins from Amman were much poorer. The latter would come to seek working opportunities or to marry one of the Israeli women of their lineage in order to settle in the Negev and have a better standard of living. For instance, when 'Abd al-Karim, Hamdan's second son, came on regular visits to the village of the Rashayde in Israel, he would be taken care of completely by his cousin 'Iyad. 'Iyad would not only offer him hospitality on his long stays, but would also find him job opportunities, negotiate his salary, and be responsible for him in case of conflict with his employers. When 'Abd al-Karim tried to find a bride for his son, he had to rely on 'Iyad who introduced to him the daughter of one of his acquaintances in a neighboring unrecognized village. Later, when the engagement failed, 'Iyad took charge of solving the litigation while preventing his cousin from interfering. In sum, while in public 'Iyad would present his Jordanian cousin as an equal, within the family, the latter would appear as his follower.

All in all, during the 1990s these widening gaps created situations in which the Bedouin became potential helpers or patrons. While people kept crossing borders, the content of their relations evolved significantly as the redrawing of borders and the changing status of partners, structurally opened a margin for stronger power relations and conflicts of interests.

Power relations and conflicts of interest. As the new security measures forced more and more Palestinians to enter Israel illegally in search of work, they became more vulnerable vis-à-vis their employers. It would be difficult or even impossible for Palestinian workers to complain to the Israeli authorities for being treated badly or not remunerated according to what they were promised by their Israeli employers. Bornstein (2002) gives a few examples showing how Israeli Arabs and Jews profited from this situation during the Oslo period in the central region of Israel. Similar cases happened in the Negev. In 2002–2003, following the tightening of control in the southern West Bank and the drastic reduction in work permits issued, Bedouin taxis reinvented themselves as "workers' smugglers" (*muharribin 'ummal*). To cover their risk, they raised their fee for a one-way trip from the Green Line to Beersheba (Rotem 2003). In 2002, in Rahat, a Bedouin town north of Beersheba, an unskilled West Bank worker would earn 100 NIS a day. The fare from Rahat to the Green Line was 50 NIS. Another van would pick the workers up from the other side of the Green Line and take them to their villages (most were from al-Dura) for 5 NIS. It was not economical to travel both directions for one day's work. There were no taxis that did both sides of this journey.[8]

Even in legal situations, the framework that emerged during the Oslo period and later opened a greater margin for exploitation. At the Erez Crossing, the Israelis and the Palestinians created a free zone where Israeli industries hired Gazan Palestinians. Little attention was paid to the working conditions in this zone.

Some of the Israeli Palestinians who invested in the Erez Zone were Bedouin from the Negev. One of them, Salim, a Bedouin living east of Beersheba, ran a sewing factory. He would purchase pieces of clothes from the Far East, assemble them at Erez and sell them to Europe or the United States. He employed more than 50 Palestinian workers, both men and women. His business was not successful, and he could not pay the workers

---

8 Discussion with Richard Ratcliffe June 2004.

on time, but the workers did not complain as they had no other job opportunities. It was not until the summer of 1998 when some kin and close relations of the workers came to Salim's factory and tried to break some machinery. Salim was not there, and his subordinates, who supervised the factory in his absence, stopped the angry relatives. The relatives threatened they would return if the wages were not paid the same day.

When informed of the incident at home, Salim reported the story to his brothers. They mobilized 10 youths from the family that went immediately to the Erez Industrial Zone. Ready to protect the family business, they brought sticks and knives. They reached Erez an hour later and entered without being questioned by the Israeli soldiers. Their arrival at the factory was a real *mise en scène* of power. The youths rustled up by Salim and his two brothers entered the factory by force threatening to beat the frightened workers gathered behind Salim's subordinate, Ahmed, who was trying to explain to them that they were not in danger as the Gazans had left earlier in the afternoon. The tension remained high for over an hour. The young Bedouin provoked the workers who intended to protest at their overdue pay. Later Salim informed them that he would not allow them to threaten him this way. Stressing his "Bedouin background," he said he would not be afraid to use force against force. In the end, the workers were paid a few months' of unpaid wages and were promised that the remaining sum of money owed them would be paid as soon as the factory began to make new profits.

Needless to say, this situation is extreme. Moreover, the action did not gain unanimous support from within the lineage. Back in Israel, Salim, his brothers and the youths who chose to accompany them were strongly criticized by the other members of his lineage. First, the elders (*kbar*) argued that in conflicts each part should try to solve it by negotiation before sending the youths (*shebab*). In addition, Salim was accused of exploiting people who did not have any other means for providing food for their families. Still, the situation shows to what extent the widening gap created by the border situation between the Bedouin and their fellow Palestinians opened cross-border relations to potentially extreme and violent relationships of power.

In the 1990s, border changes and their outcomes broadened the power gap inside trans-border kinship groups. The cross-border ties that developed between separated branches of the Rashayde were already unbalanced between the end of the 1960s and the end of the 1980s. For instance, Israeli Rashayde mainly married women from their agnates in the occupied territories while refusing to give them their own daughters and sisters to wed. At the end of the 1990s, only two grooms born in the Gaza Strip were married to Israeli women, and their marriages were explicitly conducted in order to organize their settlement in Israel. Of course, the marriage of Gazan or West Bank daughters in Israel enabled the Rashayde living in Gaza and in the region of al-Dhahriyya to avoid having to marry them outside the lineage.[9] In fact, this pattern reveals the perception of status of the different people on both sides of the border. On the one hand, the Rashayde of the occupied territories and Jordan would consider the marrying of their daughters in Israel as an opportunity to marry her to kin and eventually to provide her with a better standard of living. Israeli members, on the other hand, perceived the marriage of their daughters to Gaza, al-Dhahriyya, and Jordan as similar to a marriage with a stranger and as synonymous with downward mobility. For the latter, a close marriage would mean to marry their daughter either inside the Israeli branch, or to a groom from a neighboring group in Israel with whom they maintain close links. This distinct perception of closeness expresses the fragmented perceptions of space as well as cross-border encounters within the Rashayde.

This distinct fragmented experience and the conflicts of interests it gave rise to, grew in the late 1990s. The stronger limitations on freedom of movement and the emergence of a permit system to work in Israel gave a new pragmatic dimension to cross-border matrimonial exchanges. Giving Palestinian or Jordanian spouses the right of residency, and even citizenship, in Israel meant that cross-border matrimonial alliances became an opportunity to sidestep the entire procedure linked with obtaining work permits and thus was synonymous with prosperity. At the end of the 1990s, many Palestinian and Jordanian kin of Bedouin remained in Israel to initiate negotiations in order to marry Israeli Bedouin relatives. According to the Ministry of Interior, since 1993, the number of applications for family unifications following weddings amounted between 22,000 to 23,000 in all of Israel. According to the population registry in the Interior Ministry, every request of this kind brings an additional six more people on average. All in all, the number of Palestinians who have begun proceedings to get citizenship stood at 140,000 in 2002 (Muallem 2002; Badil 2002).

---

9 Seemingly, this strategy was shared between all the scattered branches outside of Israel. Among the descendants of 'Awad's brother, Ibrahim, all the daughters were married to agnates in Israel or in Egypt. The only daughter who was married outside the family was engaged to a Bedouin refugee in Gaza. Similarly, among the Dhahriyya descendants of 'Awad's second brother, Hamdan, all daughters were engaged with grooms from the Israeli branch. Furthermore, during this period, the members of the lineage exiled in Jordan married all their daughters to Israeli sons of their brother or patrilineal cousin, while they engaged their sons to local brides, whether Bedouin, peasants, or town dwellers.

The authorities claimed that the growth of non-Jewish population in Israel was a threat to the Jewish character of the State (Badil 2002) as well as a security danger. It is on this basis that the Israeli government decided to freeze such procedures in 2002. In 2003, as noted above, the Knesset voted for a resolution to forbid Palestinian spouses the right to obtain residency or citizenship. Interior Minister Avraham Poraz argued that it was necessary as "during the *intifada* there has been growing involvement in terrorism of Palestinians who are residents of the territories and have Israeli ID cards as a result of family reunification or marriage, exploiting their status as Israelis to move freely between Israel and the territories" (Alon 2003).

In addition, such alliances became a problematic issue among the Bedouin. In a few cases, Palestinian spouses divorced their Israeli wives as soon as they obtained the right of residency or citizenship. However rare, these few cases were enough to spread the rumor and frighten the Israeli Bedouin. To prevent such a risk, Bedouin fathers raised the second part of the *mahir*, the *muta'ajjal*,[10] thus obliging the spouse to give a significant sum of money in case of divorce. In some cases, I witnessed people asking for a *muta'ajjal* of up to $50,000. Among the Israeli Rashayde, some people even refused to give the hand of their daughters to their Jordanian kin.

Recently, the harsher limitations on movement and the worsening political situation have prevented Palestinians and Jordanians from marrying their daughters to Israeli kin. The policy of closure made such alliances more threatening to Palestinians as it meant that parents would be cut off from their daughters. Not only would they have difficulties in visiting her, but they would also have no possibility to protect her from potential abuse by her husband or his kin. Another motivation for this new tendency may have come from the fact that during the 1960s and 1970s, many Palestinian and Jordanian Bedouin men married local women, whose mothers would be less interested in marrying their daughters into the family of their husbands across the border. Like the Israeli Bedouin, they preferred to marry their daughters within physical proximity rather than within the lineage.

Altogether these new developments struck a sharp blow to cross-border alliances. Among the Rashayde, they dwindled compared to the past. Between 1990 and 2003, seven marriages where concluded: two between with Gazan Rashayde (one girl and one boy), two with Jordanian Rashayde

---

10 The *mahir* is often translated as the bridal price. It is the compensation given by the groom's family to the family of the bride. It is composed of two parts. First, there is the *muta'ajjal* or *mutagaddim* that is given immediately to the bride's family; second, there is the *muta'ajjal* or *muta'akhir*, that is an agreed sum given to the bride if she is repudiated by her husband.

(two girls), and three with West Bank Rashayde (three girls). They amount to one fifth of the total number of marriages in the Rashayde lineage during this period, as compared to one third in the 1980s.

Feelings of difference and inequalities, as well as conflicts of interest were sharpened by the deterioration in the general political situation over the last 15 years. During the two *intifadas*, as well as during the Oslo period, loyalties were put to test more than ever. Like the other Palestinian Israelis, the Bedouin were victims of a double suspicion: their Jewish neighbors always considered them part of a fifth column (*gays khameshi* [Hebrew]), while their fellow Palestinians were similarly wary.

One day in spring 2001, 'Iyad was invited to Muthgal's house in al-Dhahriyya to meet with PNA officials. After less than half an hour, one of them started to ask 'Iyad why young Bedouin enrolled in the Israeli army. He also expressed his disappointment for the lack of mobilization of the Bedouin in September 2000, when the second *intifada* began, while he was impressed by the mobilization of Palestinian Israelis in the Galilee. 'Iyad said the Bedouin were afraid, and that they depended on Jews more than the Arab population in Galilee did. An uprising in the Negev would have severed the links between Jews and the Bedouin, attracting the anger of the Israeli authorities. Regarding the military service, he said it concerned only a minority of people, mostly uneducated, and frightened by the authorities. He did not mention the fact that three years earlier, he had decided to send his own son to the army with the blessing of his Palestinian cousin Muthgal. After the two Palestinian officials left, 'Iyad complained to his cousins, Muthgal and his brother Sami. He argued that the attitude was unjust, especially from Palestinian officials whom he accused of using their powerful positions to get rich at the expense of their own people. His cousins made a point to agree with him, as they measured his frustration. Nevertheless, they could hardly hide their assent with their two Palestinians guests. Such encounters were bitter experiences that 'Iyad would discuss later with his Israeli kin, back inside the Green Line. Like many other Palestinian Israelis, he would feel held back by his difference.

Conclusion

Rather than challenging the borders, trans-border exchanges adjusted to them. During the last 50 years, exchanges between the Negev Bedouin and their kin and network in the Gaza Strip, the West Bank, and Jordan, evolved in accordance with border policies. From 1967 until 1994, exchanges were intense and regular as no obstacle stood in their way, but their intensity and their content changed significantly in the late 1990s due to the imposition of new security measures.

Throughout this period, trans-border exchanges created an intricate web of relationships extending social, economic, and political spaces of the population involved. In the case of the Rashayde lineage, such contacts gave rise to trans-border kinship groups that constituted the basis for the emergence of trans-border groups of solidarity and interest as well as trans-border configurations of power. Together with economic partnerships, these exchanges fostered the passage of goods, people, and values, leading to a sharing of culture. Further, these cross-borders encounters question sharp distinctions established by scholars between the Bedouin and their Palestinian kin and networks. Such a web of intricate relations makes difficult the dissociation of discrete cultures or societies separated by the Green Line or international borders.

However, even the broadening of the space of relations of local population does not constitute a challenge for such borders as they are not necessarily meant to separate people. Since 1967, the border policies of successive Israeli governments enabled flows of people on both sides of the Green Line. Even during the Oslo period and later, during the second *intifada*, Israel only tightened its control over the movement of people rather than stopping it. From this perspective, the emergence of an intricate web of relationship across the Green Line follows the logic of such policies rather than challenging it.

Furthermore, cross-border relations do not erase boundaries between the populations involved. As we noticed, while people cross the Green Line or the international border with Jordan, they carry with them existing boundaries or create new ones. Occurring in an unequal framework of relationships, exchanges across borders are moments and places where people experience their differences and develop antagonisms. This process has become all the more acute in the last 15 years. Widening gaps on the legal and economic levels strengthened relationships of power and gave rise to conflicts. Border encounters are often marked by bitter or violent experiences, creating mistrust and sometimes fear. They foster feelings of differences and fragmented experience between cross-border partners.

Practiced on a daily basis, and over a long period of time, these differences and antagonisms are internalized and often perceived as a given. This is all the more true as people use these experiences to reconstruct dominant narratives that stress distinctions between these very populations. Each experience is added to other stories that people heard or witnessed personally. Narratives about "us" and the "others" are often presented as facts; they are built upon an accumulation of multiple stories about ourselves and others (Vila 2003:107; van Dijk 1993:126). These cross-border encounters and the experiences people draw from them validate categories like, "Bedouin" against "Palestinians," whether "West Banker" (*dhaffawi*) or "Gazan" (*ghazzawi*). In brief, while trans-border encounters favor strong ties as well as a sharing of culture, they also foster processes of differentiation already at work among local populations. This is the case for the processes of ethnicization and community-building undergone by the Bedouin who remained in the Negev. Instead of questioning their isolation from their Palestinian neighbors, border encounters nourish their feelings of difference towards the latter.

Trans-border networks tie the Bedouin to their fellow Palestinians while re-adjusting their relations in the framework imposed by border policies. The analysis of the matrimonial alliances developed by the Rashayde over the last 35 years shows to what extend such exchanges can define and sanction new hierarchies between the groups involved. Throughout this period, the Israeli Rashayde imposed themselves as women "takers" while their relatives on the other side of the Green Line and the international border with Jordan were forced into the role of women "givers." This outcome is all the more significant once we take into consideration the hierarchical implications of such a pattern in the Arab marriage (Bonte and Conte 1991; Kressel 1992). In addition to this, we can witness the deepening of relationships of power that takes place on the economic level.

From this perspective, cross-border exchanges do not merely adjust to the power of borders, but also re-adjust their power on the ground. They sanction and deepen inequalities between cross-border partners, whether in terms of status or in terms of apprehending the space. The implications of such trans-border networks are huge for envisaging any potential Palestinian return migration: for some people, networks or social relations may be more significant than physical place.

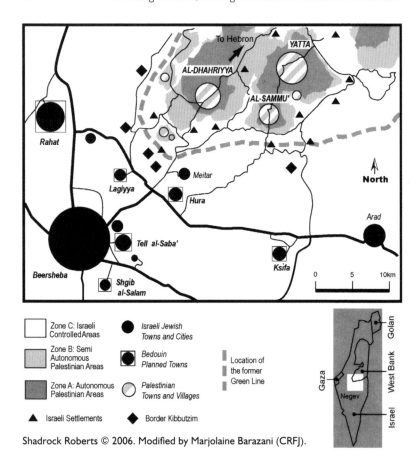

Figure 1: **Northern Negev (Israel) and Southern Hebron Hills (West Bank) before the Second Intifada (September 2000)**

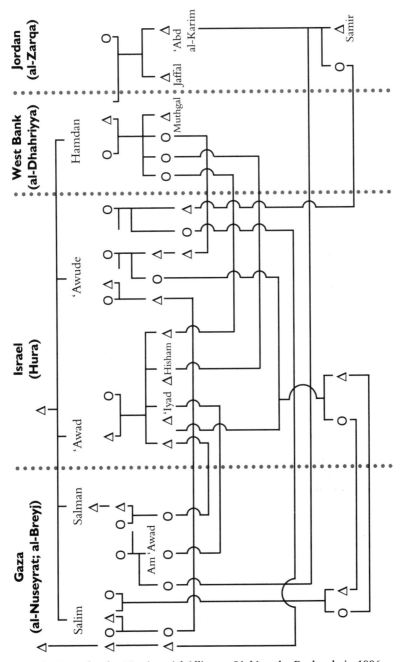

Figure 2: **Cross-border Matrimonial Alliances Linking the Rashayde in 1996**

Bibliography

Abu Rabia, 'Arif. 1994. *The Negev Bedouin and Livestock Rearing: Social, Economic and Political Aspects*. Oxford: Berg Publishers.

———. 2000. "Employment and Unemployment among the Negev Bedouin," *Nomadic People*, 4(2):84–94.

Alon, Gideon. 2003. "Knesset forbids citizenship to Palestinians who marry Israelis," June, 18, *Ha'aretz*, (http://www.haaretz.com).

Arnon, Arie, Israel Luski, and Jimmy Weinblatt. 1997. *The Palestinian Economy: Between Imposed Integration and Voluntary Separation*. Leiden: Brill.

Badil Resource Center. 2002. *The "Demographic Nightmare,"* Press Release, May 21.

Barth, Fredrik. 1995. "Les groupes ethniques et leurs frontières." In Ph. Poutignat, and J. Streiff-Fenart, *Théories de l'ethnicité*. Paris: PUF. (See Fredrik Barth, *Ethnic Groups and Boundaries*. Oslo: Universitetsforlaget, 1969.)

Bar-Zvi, Sasson. 1991. *Masoret hashiput shel bedui hanegev*. Tel Aviv: Ministry of Defense (Hebrew).

Basson, Lauren. 1995. "Les Bédouins du Néguev et l'Etat d'Israël," *Monde arabe, Maghreb Machrek*, 147 (janvier–mars):149–165.

Bonte, Pierre and Edouard Conte. 1991. "La tribu arabe. Approches anthropologiques et orientalistes." in P. Bonte, E. Conte, C. Hamès, and A.W. Ould Cheikh, eds., *Al-Ansab: La quête des origines. Anthropologie historique de la société tribale arabe*. Paris: Maison des Sciences de l'Homme.

Bornstein, Avram. 2002. *Crossing the Green Line Between the West Bank and Israel*. Philadelphia: University of Pennsylvania Press.

Burns, E. L. M. 1962. *Between Arab and Israeli*. London and Toronto: George G. Harrap.

Dinero, Steve. 1997. "Female Role Change and Male Response in Post Nomadic Urban Environments: The Case of the Israeli Negev Bedouin," *Journal of Comparative Family Studies*, vol. XXVIII (3):248–61.

Al-Hamamde, Farraj Sliman. 1996. "Turath waqada' 'asha'ir 'arab an-naqab." Unpublished manuscript.

Farsakh, Leila. 2002. "Palestinian Labor Flows to the Israeli Economy: a Finished Story?" *Journal of Palestine Studies*, 32(1):13–27.

———. 2005. *Palestinian Labour Migration to Israel: Labour, Land and Occupation*. London: Routledge.

Hannerz, Ulf. 1997. "Borders," *International Social Science Journal*, 154:537–548.

Jakubowska, Longina. 1985. "Urban Bedouin: Social Change in a Settled Environment." PhD Thesis, The State University of New York: Stony Brook

———. 1992. "Resisting Ethnicity: The Israeli State and Bedouin Ethnicity." In C. Nordstrom, and J. Martin, eds., *The Paths to Domination and Terror*. Berkeley: University of California Press.

Kressel, Gideon M. 1975. *Pratiyut le'umat shivtiyut* (Individual versus Tribality). Hakibutz: Hameuhad.

——. 1992. *Descent through Males: An Anthropological Investigation into Patterns Underlying Social Hierarchy, Kinship, and Marriage among Former Bedouin in the Ramla-Lod Area (Israel).* Mediterranean Language and Culture Monograph Series 8. Wiesbaden: Harrassowitz.

——. 1993. "Nomadic Pastoralists, Agriculturists and the State: Self-Sufficiency and Dependence in the Middle East," *Journal of Cooperation,* 21 (1):33–49.

Legrain, Jean-François.1997. "Palestine: Les bantoustans d'Allah." In R. Bocco, B. Destremau, and J. Hannoyer, eds., *Palestine, Palestiniens: territoire national, espaces communautaires.* Beirut: CERMOC.

Lewando-Hundt, G. 1978. "Women's Power and Settlement: The Effect of Settlement on the Position of Negev Bedouin Women." MA Thesis, University of Edinburgh.

Lustick, Ian. 1980. *Arabs in the Jewish State. Israel's Control of a National Minority. Modern Middle East Studies,* 6. Austin: University of Texas Press.

Marx, Emanuel. 1967. *Bedouin of the Negev.* Manchester: Manchester University Press.

——. 1974. *Hahevra Habeduit Banegev.* Tel Aviv: Rasafim.

——. 2000. "Land and Work: Negev Bedouin Struggle with Israeli Bureaucracies," *Nomadic Peoples* 4 (2):107–121.

Meir, Avinoam.1996. *As Nomadism Ends: The Israeli Bedouin of the Negev.* Boulder: Westview Press.

Morris, Benny. 1997. *The Birth of the Palestinian Refugee Problem, 1947–1949.* Cambridge: Cambridge University Press.

Muallem, Mazal. 2003. "Yishai seeks to cut non-Jewish citizenship," March, 27, *Ha'aretz,* (http://www.haaretz.com).

Parizot, Cédric.1999. "Enjeux tribaux et élections nationales," *REMMM* 85–86:237–58.

——. 2001a. "Gaza, Beer Sheva, Dahriyya: Une autre approche des Bédouins du Néguev dans l'espace israélo-palestinien," *Bulletin du Centre de recherche français de Jérusalem* 9:37–50.

——. 2001b. *Le mois de la bienvenue.* PhD Thesis (Thèse de doctorat nouveau régime). Paris: EHESS.

Rekhess, Elie, ed. 1996. *The Arab Politics in Israel at a Crossroads.* Occasional Papers, 119. Tel Aviv: Moshe Dayan Center for Middle Eastern and African Studies.

Rotem, Tsahar. 2003. "The Gaping Hole in the South," August 28, *Ha'aretz,* p.3.

Shohat, Moshe and Yosif Ben David. 2000. *At-turath al-hadari libedu fi an-naqab* (Education Administration for the Bedouin in the Negev). Jerusalem: Jerusalem Institute for Israel Research.

Tamari, Salim. 1997. "Social Science Research in Palestine: a Review of Trends and Issues." In R. Bocco, B. Destremau, and J. Hannoyer, eds., *Palestine, Palestiniens: Territoire National, Espaces Communautaires*. Beirut: CERMOC.

UN Human Rights Committee. 2003. *"Information Sheet # 3, Family Unification and Citizenship,"* July, 22, (www.adalah.org/eng/intladvocacy/unhrc_03_fam_uni. pdf).

Van Dijk, Teun A. 1993. "Stories and Racism." In D.K. Mumby, ed., *Narrative and Social Control: Critical Perspectives*. Newbury Park, California: Sage.

Vila, Pablo. 2003. "Conclusion: The Limits of American Border Theory." In P. Vila, ed., *Ethnography at the Border*. Minneapolis: University of Minnesota Press.

Yiftachel, Oren. 1996. "Politics of Judaization," *Constellations* 6(3):364–390.

Chapter 5

Itineraries of Palestinian Refugees

Kinship as Resource in Emigration

Mohamed Kamel Doraï

A social world is not confined to a particular place or limited by territorial boundaries. Some of the relationships may be very important, but physically distant, while others may be almost insignificant although located close by. What is important is which social relationships play a role in a particular situation. (Marx 1990:194)

Introduction: The Development of Emigration

TODAY, even if some Palestinians are still forced to move from their place of residence (e.g. Palestinians expelled from Kuwait in 1991, from Libya in 1995, and inside the occupied territories), Palestinian migration develops inside the Diaspora on a more or less "voluntary" basis, connecting distant poles such as North America or Europe. Parallel to this "voluntary migration" movement, a "forced return" movement occurred. For example, Palestinians who migrated to Iraq to work and study had to leave because of war and its economic and political consequences. These different types of migration obey regional and state constraints as well as dynamics generated by the Palestinians themselves and rely upon migratory networks set up on local and familial bases. Studies of Palestinian refugees, one of the oldest refugee communities in the world, could contribute to the growing interest on integrating refugee studies to the wider field of migration theory (Koser 2002).

This paper deals with the situation of the Palestinian refugees in Lebanon. Since the 1970s, more than 100,000 Palestinians,[1] about 25 percent of the total Palestinian population residing in Lebanon, have emigrated from Lebanon to the Gulf countries and Northern Europe, mainly Germany, Sweden, and Denmark. Considering the organization of Palestinian emigration from Lebanon to Europe, from the 1960s to today, and particularly the migratory networks from the Tyre region in Lebanon to Europe and Iraq, and based on interviews with refugees in south Lebanon and Sweden, a certain picture emerges. Until 1987, many Palestinians fled Lebanon and obtained refugee status in Europe. During the 1970s and the 1980s, a smaller group of Palestinians also went to work and study in Iraq. After 1987, Europe gradually closed its borders to Palestinian refugees, while the situation in Lebanon grew worse. The community tensions in Lebanon, which were exacerbated during the Lebanese civil war, culminated in 1985–1987 with the war of the camps.[2] The Amal militia tried to make Palestinians flee the Tyre area, which the former wanted to make a Shiite canton. A large majority of Palestinians did indeed flee towards Sidon, the nearest Sunni city, but most of them came back to Tyre at the end of the Lebanese civil war in 1991. During the 1990s, four main factors led to the development of emigration: (1) the end of the civil war in Lebanon increased the discrimination against the Palestinian community at the political and economic levels, (2) the Oslo agreement did not provide any solution, nor any prospects for one, for the 1948 refugees, (3) the economic situation in Lebanon was getting worse in 1993, and (4) Palestinians were competing with Syrian and Egyptian workers in the labor market. In the absence of the implementation of their "right of return," Palestinians from Lebanon looked for a better economic situation, a recognized legal status, and a country where they could build a "normal" life for their children. On a regional scale, due to war, tension and economic closures, Iraq became less

---

1 In his statistical overview of Palestinians in Lebanon, Razqallah (1998) gives the number of 100,000 Palestinians from Lebanon living abroad in the mid 1990s. This estimation fits the statistics available on Palestinians in Europe, where about 18,000 Palestinians live in Sweden in 2006 (see Migrationsverket 2002, www.migrationsverket.se); 12,000 in Denmark (Danish Immigration Service 2001, www.nyidanmark.dk); probably 30,000 in Germany (this last number is a personal estimation based on interviews). The majority of these Palestinians hold Lebanese travel documents. The rest of the Palestinians from Lebanon who live abroad are settled in Arab oil producing countries. However, since most of the recent emigration towards Europe is illegal, it is very difficult to give reliable figures on actual Palestinian emigration from Lebanon since the 1990s.

2 Between the Shiite Lebanese militia Amal and the Palestinian refugee camp dwellers.

attractive to new Arab immigrants. Palestinians already settled there began to face not only economic difficulties but also discrimination.

The 1982 Israeli invasion triggered Palestinian emigration from Lebanon, but this alone can neither explain its duration nor its size. This paper will analyze how Palestinian refugees, deprived of passport and financial resources, have managed to leave their country of residence and enter Western Europe. One of the key hypotheses is the following: Palestinian refugees in the refugee camps and the informal settlements in Lebanon have reconstructed systems of solidarity based on kinship and local networks.[3] These networks, developed at a local level, have been turned into transnational networks of solidarity by migrant communities, building bridges between Palestinians in Lebanon and migrants abroad. Resources such as money, information on destination countries, legal constraints or opportunities, circulate through these networks, linking potential migrants to Palestinians settled in Europe. These networks facilitate refugees' mobility, in a context of difficult legal constraints in Europe, and a lack of financial resources in Lebanon. Palestinians had to organize themselves to get around those difficulties. They used their transnational resources, such as their close contacts with the Palestinian communities living abroad and the migratory networks they constructed in the 1980s, to facilitate emigration. Transnationalism developed by Palestinian refugees has to be considered mainly as a strategy to escape a highly restrictive regional environment, especially in Lebanon. Migratory networks, based on family ties, are also one of the few resources accessible to return migrants who were forced to leave Iraq and come back to Lebanon without international assistance.

This paper is divided into two parts: the first will explore, in a theoretical perspective, the usefulness of analyzing the diversity of migratory refugee experiences and the building of transnational networks; and the second will present different migratory itineraries collected during various fieldwork trips in Lebanon to show the different use of transnational networks and access to resources.

Towards a Comprehensive Approach to Palestinian Diaspora Migration

Many studies on Palestinian refugees have explored the fields of memory (e.g. Khalidi 1991) and national formation (e.g. Brand 1998). More recently, with

---

3   Informal settlements are unofficial refugee camps, built up by the refugees themselves, mostly on private Lebanese land without authorization of Lebanese authorities. Most of them are concentrated in rural areas.

the beginning of the peace process in 1991, research has been conducted on the refugee question, their legal status, and their number (Abu-Sitta 2001; Tamari 1996; Zureik 1996). Only a few studies have been published on the new forms of social organization in the Palestinian refugee communities abroad (e.g. Hanafi 2001; Radi 1995). Nevertheless, the diversity and the complexity of refugee experiences have to be explored.

From refugees to migrants? Network analysis provides an interesting framework that goes beyond the juridical analysis, imposed by the term "refugee" itself whose origin is deeply rooted in international law. The Palestinian experience is a good illustration of this. More than 50 years of exile have generated a wide range of different situations, from stateless refugees still living in poor refugee camps in Middle East countries to rich investors holding Gulf or Western citizenship. A huge diversity of social, legal, and economic statuses and personal backgrounds co-exist inside the category "Palestinian refugee." As Liisa Malkki (1995:496) pointed out:

> "Refugees" do not constitute a naturally self-delimiting domain of anthropological knowledge. Forced population movements have extraordinarily diverse historical and political causes and involve people who, while all displaced, find themselves in qualitatively different situations and predicaments. Thus, it would seem that the term "refugee" has analytical usefulness not as a label for a special, generalizable "kind" or "type" of person or situation, but only as a broad legal or descriptive rubric that includes within it a world of different socioeconomic statuses, personal histories, and psychological or spiritual situations. Involuntary or forced movements of people are always only one aspect of much larger constellations of sociopolitical and cultural processes and practices.

Refugees and migration theories. Early attempts to build a general theoretical model of refugee issues have focused mainly on *push* factors to explain refugee movements (Kunz 1973, 1981). More recent studies have emphasized the role of international relations in the production of refugee flows (Loescher 1990; Weiner 1993). If *push* factors as well as international politics are key issues for the understanding of refugee movements, little attention has been paid to dynamics generated by the refugees themselves. The duration of exile and the different kind of interactions with the host societies have also generated different forms of mobility. Richmond (1994:55) stresses that:

> ... *the distinction between free and forced or voluntary and invol-*
> *untary is a misleading one. All human behavior is constrained.*
> *Choices are not unlimited but are determined by the structuration*
> *process. However, degrees of freedom may vary. Individual and group*
> *autonomy and potency are situationally determined. It would be more*
> *appropriate to recognize a continuum at one end of which individuals*
> *and collectivities are proactive and at the other reactive.*

Seteney Shami (1993:12) notes that in the Middle East this distinction between forced migration and voluntary migration is not always relevant. The author suggests that "displacement often leads to labor migration as a coping strategy." Palestinian emigration from Lebanon fits this analytical framework. First, Palestinians are considered as refugees in Lebanon because they were expelled from their homeland in 1948, and they are recognized as refugees both by UNRWA and the Lebanese state. Then, the Lebanese civil war, economic difficulties, and legal discrimination[4] have led them to emigrate from Lebanon to find work, asylum and/or a stable juridical status in Europe or in other Arab countries, especially oil-producing countries. Palestinian emigration from Lebanon cannot be considered only as forced, but also as the result of new forms of transnational migration between the different scattered Palestinian communities. Interaction with the host society, namely the Lebanese one, is also a key factor in understanding Palestinian emigration. Moreover the important Lebanese emigration for more then one century to South and North America as well as Africa,[5] is a central element to take into consideration while studying Palestinian migratory movements.

The emergence of migratory networks: "Forced" transnationalism?[6] Network analysis of migration is a growing field of interest that developed in the early 1990s after a beginning in the 1970s (see Durand 1994; Fawcett 1989; Kritz and Zlotnik 1992, Massey et al. 1988).[7] Thomas Faist (2000) observes that the analysis of migrations in terms of migratory networks suffers from one main deficiency: it does not tackle the question of

---

4 See, for example, al-Natour (1997) and Said (2001).

5 See, for example, Hourani and Shehadi (1992).

6 This expression has been used by Michael P. Smith (2002: xiii) who stresses that studies on "refugee diasporas, has produced such new and useful conceptual categories as ambivalent transnationalism and even 'forced' transnationalism."

7 For a synthetic approach of network analysis related to migration see, E. Ma Mung (1998).

the emergence of the migratory networks. He considers that initially social capital[8] is a factor that limits mobility, then, when the migratory networks develop, it becomes a driving force of emigration. This analytical framework is relevant to understanding Palestinian migratory dynamics from Lebanon to Europe. Until 1982, Palestinian refugees in Lebanon were not very mobile because of the strength of the solidarity networks and mutual aid, based on family and/or local networks, which developed in the camps and the informal settlements. The destruction of these camps during the Israeli invasion of 1982 led to the departure of many refugees towards Northern Europe. New forms of solidarity then developed in a transnational migratory field,[9] which supported and accelerated the emigration. Thomas Faist also notes that the installation of earlier migrants is a central element that permits the development of migratory networks because they condense the social capital. Migration develops when social capital does not function only on a local scale, but also as a transnational transmission belt.

In recent years, the relation between refugees and transnationalism has been the subject of investigation (Shami 1996; al-Ali et al. 2001; Black 2001; Koser 2002; Wahlbeck 2002). Studies conducted on refugees' transnational activities have contributed to address the role of the state in shaping migrants' networks in a more comprehensive way, and bringing the state back into most of these analyses. As noted by Richard Black (2001:66):

> *Focusing on the role played by refugees in transnational activities could help to dispel some of the more idealistic notions of transnationalism from below as a people-led process, which takes advantage of processes of globalization and ease of travel in the modern world.*

Even if Palestinians are involved in transnational practices in order to adapt to a new environment in Lebanon and Europe, they are still refugees—and/or asylum seekers—strongly tributary to the political context in the Middle East and asylum policies in Europe. State policies toward refugees remain one

---

8   Thomas Faist (2000:15) defines social capital as follows: "Social capital denotes the transactions between individuals and groups that facilitate social action, and the benefits derived from these mechanisms. It is primarily a local asset and can be transferred cross-nationally only under specific conditions."

9   "The migratory field is defined as the whole space structured by migratory and relational flows, a space that is travelled through, frequented, lived by the migrant population" ["Le champ migratoire est, ici, défini comme l'ensemble de l'espace structuré par les flux migratoires et relationnels, espace parcouru, pratiqué, vécu par les populations migrantes"] (Simon 2000).

of the most important elements in the understanding of refugee movements, their socio-economic status, and the viability of migratory networks both in sending and receiving countries. For the Palestinian refugees, their transnational activities are strongly determined by the attitude of their departure and destination countries, as mentioned by Östen Wahlbeck (2002:228):

> *It can be argued that the social relations of refugees create a transnational community not bound by the geographical borders of either the countries of origin or the countries of settlement…. However, there are some significant differences between ordinary migrants and refugees in the form and content of the transnational social relations. It can be argued that refugees have a distinctive relationship with both the country they have been forced to flee from and the country in which they have involuntarily settled.*

The factors that led to the setting up and development of these transnational migratory networks are the following: Until the beginning of the 1980s, the restrictive legal context which affected the Palestinians in Lebanon was counterbalanced by the density of kinship solidarity networks at a local scale—refugee camps and informal settlements—and the strong presence of the PLO. The Palestinian institutions provided work and welfare to the most underprivileged Palestinians. The Palestinian national movement, then strongly structured, also proposed a political solution to the refugees by making the "right of return" its combat slogan. The dismantling of the PLO and its geographical dispersion in 1982, and more recently the collapse of the peace process, reduced the effectiveness of the networks of solidarity at a local level. Emigration became the only solution for many refugees, because it made possible an escape from a situation perceived as intractable by most of them. Emigrating was considered by refugees as an alternative solution to an increasingly improbable return to their homeland or to a permanent settlement in Lebanon in an increasingly hostile context. This emigration relies mainly upon kinship networks.[10]

Kinship networks and the transnational migration process. Relations between migratory networks and kinship have already been developed by many authors, concerning "economic" migrants, such as Algerians in France and more specifically with the development of family reunification in

---

10 I will not emphasize here the role of village networks, which partly include kinship networks. For a more detailed approach on this topic see Doraï (2003a).

western countries (Montagne 1954; Choldin 1973; Katuszewski and Ogien 1981; Boyd 1989; Fawcett 1989). Some researchers in the refugee studies field have also pointed out the importance of family networks in the adaptation to host countries of forced migrants (e.g., Hansen 1981). But little attention has been paid to kinship as a key element of the migration process of refugee communities.

Palestinian refugees provide an interesting and singular case study. They are one of the oldest stateless refugee communities, recognized as such, where a significant proportion still lives in refugee camps and informal settlements.[11] Their geographic concentration, as well as their legal and political status in Arab host countries, has led to the permanence and/or the reinforcement of kinship networks in exile as one of the cores of diasporic social organization. Kinship networks are one of the few resources accessible to refugees deprived of their basic rights (Doraï 2000; Doraï and Doraï 2002).

The kinship solidarity networks play a significant role in the organization and development of Palestinian migrations, in both the country of departure and the host country. Their action is determined by various stages of a migratory process: (1) they permit the mobilization of the funds necessary to pay for the trip, (2) they provide information on the country of destination circulated through the network and spread to potential migrants, (3) they facilitate the adaptation of the newcomer in the host country, (4) they also play a role in the selection of the migrant from the departure country to fit the specific needs of the host country, (5) they contribute to the circumvention of the legal constraints in the host countries, and (6) they influence the choice of destination of migrants (Gurak and Caces 1992; Boyd 1989; Light et al. 1993). Transnational migratory networks set up by Palestinian refugees, based on family and village solidarity, are built on the same logic that helped the networks of sociability develop on a local scale in the refugee camps and at Palestinian gatherings. It is a geographical extension from these networks, from a local to a transnational field. The Palestinians who were settled in Europe since the 1960s were used as a spearhead for the migratory networks, which developed in the 1980s. This migratory strategy has been developed to circumvent the legal border closures in Europe. This phenomenon can also be observed for Palestinians going to Iraq, but in a less systematic way, due to the legal possibility of circulating between Lebanon and Iraq.

---

11 In June 2003, 57 percent of the registered refugees in Lebanon were living in one of the 12 refugee camps according to UNRWA figures. There is no official data on those living in informal settlements. According to Mahmoud Abbas (1997) and PCBS figures (al-Madi 1996) and personal estimates, a total of 38,000 Palestinians live in such settlements, that is to say nearly 10 percent of the total Palestinian population.

Migratory Itineraries of Palestinian Refugees

Family migratory networks constitute the main support for the emigration from Lebanon to Northern Europe, as well as the only resource for Palestinian return migrants from Iraq. In the Palestinian case, they play a significant role in four principal fields: collection of the funds necessary to emigrate, the "family reunification" migratory strategy, information flow between country of destination and country of departure, and the adaptation of the newcomers and/or the returnees. This point is raised by Nicholas Van Hear (2006:10):

> As scholars of transnationalism have been arguing for some time now, people at home and abroad may operate in a single social field, or at least in linked social fields. This applies as much in the context of forced migration as with other forms of migration. What was a single household in a conflict area may subsequently have members "at home" in the country of origin; in neighbouring countries of first asylum; and in the wider diaspora, in countries of asylum and resettlement: we might term this a transnational household.

I will reconstitute through five migratory itineraries the importance of the networks, and more specifically kinship networks, in the Palestinian migration process. These itineraries are reconstituted through interviews collected during fieldwork in south Lebanon from May 1999 to June 2003. Networks are often considered as something that exists, without offering empirical evidence of their existence or concrete cases of their way of functioning.

Case One: Family Migration

The story of Ayman[12] is a common one, but it points both to the strength of family ties and their limits due to restrictive state policies. Ayman's father emigrated from South Lebanon to Iraq in 1979. He was working for a Lebanese company. He moved back and forth, staying in Iraq for short periods. In 1981, he found a stable job in Iraq and decided to stay there because incomes were higher. He managed to bring his family from Lebanon the same year. They rented an apartment in Baghdad where he used to work. At this time, Palestinian refugees were granted residency permits and were allowed to work. Ayman arrived in Iraq when he was nine years old. He went to school, like all his brothers and sisters. They have all graduated from the University of Baghdad. In 1991, after the Gulf War, his father lost his job,

---

12 All the names used in this paper are pseudonyms.

and restrictions on Palestinian rights—as well as on other Arabs and foreigners—were enforced. Ayman's brother, who was an engineer, went to Abu Dhabi and found work there. His father also tried to find a job there, but incomes were too low to support a family, so he decided to stay in Iraq. The whole family lived on the remittances sent by Ayman's brother during this period, about $200 to $300 per month. When asked why they did not choose to leave Baghdad and come back to Lebanon after 1991, Ayman's father answered: "All my children were studying at the university at this period. In Iraq, education was cheap and open to Arab students. Here in Lebanon, it would have been impossible. Fees are too expensive for Palestinians. So we decided to stay there until they all got their diplomas."

Until 2000, Ayman's family rented an apartment for $30 a month, and the money sent by his brother was sufficient to live on. But by 2001, rent increased dramatically for foreigners, and shot up to $150 a month. His younger sister graduated in 2001. His parents decided to come back to Lebanon, since living in Baghdad had become both more difficult and more expensive. In Lebanon, they settled in al-Buss camp where Ayman's grandmother had a house. Ayman decided not to come back with his family because he had just married an Iraqi. He tried to find a job in the Baghdad hotels, but faced discrimination: "Once I entered an hotel and I asked for a job, the manager told me: Why do you look for a job here in Iraq? Aren't you Palestinian? Why don't you go back to your country? You have signed the Gaza and Jericho agreement."

He moved with his wife from Baghdad to Mosul, her city of origin where life was cheaper and where he could find help from his wife's relatives. He found a precarious job as a dried fruit salesman. Until 2002, he could get his residency permit because his wife was Iraqi. In 2003, when he asked to renew his permit, he was told that the law had changed and that he had to first obtain a work contract, then ask for a residency permit. He managed to find a work contract in Mosul but never got the residency permit. In February of that year, he had to leave Iraq with his wife and two children and come back to Lebanon. He went to his family's house in al-Buss camp, the only place he could live. However, he did not find a job. As a Palestinian refugee in Lebanon, he was not allowed to work.[13] He tried to find a job

---

13 Palestinian refugees face huge difficulties in entering the Lebanese labor market. *The prohibition for Palestinians from occupying certain job functions originates in the ministerial decree dated December 15, 1995, [that is] itself an update of previous decrees, the first being apparently decree 1/289 dated December 18, 1982.... The list given by the ministerial decree of December, 1995, of the salaried professions reserved to the Lebanese workforce by the Ministry of Labor, is long: 72 jobs and professions according to some people and 46 to others, such as hairdresser, concierge, cook, pharmacist, accountant, teacher, as well as other independent professions.* (FIDH 2003)
A more detailed analysis of the legal context is in al-Natour (1997).

in Beirut and in other cities in Lebanon. His wife, as an Iraqi citizen, had to pay for a residency permit and has to ask for a work permit to be allowed to work. Both of them are unemployed, like all Ayman's family who came back to Lebanon. Ayman, as a Palestinian refugee, is not entitled to obtain any kind of aid from the UN High Commission on Refugees, and his wife is also not considered a refugee because she left Iraq and entered Lebanon as Ayman's spouse.

Ayman's story clearly illustrates the complexity of refugee migrations. He left Lebanon for family reunification purposes after his father emigrated because he found a better position in Iraq. In periods of heightened restrictions and difficulties, Palestinians are often rejected as their refugee status conflicts with state policies, as was the case with this family. Thus, they went back in Lebanon as refugees seeking a country where they would be allowed to reside. Family networks can be the main motive of emigration, but it also remains the main mechanism of adjustment in case of difficulties (e.g., joblessness and looking for accommodation). When state protection is absent, as is the case in Iraq since 1991, or in Lebanon, the only resource accessible to refugees—whose basic rights are denied—is family solidarity.

Case Two: From Economic Migration to Refuge

Ahmed's case slightly differs from that of Ayman. In the early 1970s, Ahmed left Lebanon to study in Iraq, like many other young Palestinian students. He settled in Baghdad and studied civil engineering. After he obtained his diploma he decided to stay in Iraq, where job opportunities were better than in Lebanon. He first worked in an Iraqi company as an engineer, and then later he opened a small business. During this period, he was going back and forth from Iraq to Lebanon to visit his family but also for trade. When asked if he sent remittances to his family in the Rashidiyyeh camp in South Lebanon after 1982, when the situation was getting difficult there, he responded that he had never sent money and that he regretted his attitude. He met his wife—a Palestinian with Jordanian citizenship—in a Palestinian organization in Iraq. She too had come to study. They married and settled in Baghdad. He then directed his trade also towards Jordan. In 1991, the situation became more difficult and he had to stop his trade business since circulation was getting very difficult. After a short stint of unemployment, he re-opened a small shop selling leather goods. He managed to survive as a result of trade with Jordan. During the 1990s, the social and economic situation for Palestinians in Iraq was getting hard, but he did not consider going back to Lebanon where things were even worse. In 2003, when the war began, he left Baghdad with his wife because it was no longer safe. He first decided to go to Jordan, but the Jordanian border was closed to refugees and many Palestinians had been detained at the border and were not allowed to enter (Doraï et al. 2003). After several attempts, he managed to cross the Syrian border and enter Lebanon.

He returned to his family's house in Rashidiyyeh, the only place he could reside. His wife, as a Jordanian citizen, has to pay an annual fee for her residency permit. Because she does not have enough money, she never leaves the refugee camp to avoid any police checkpoints. Together, they have opened, with the help of Ahmed's family, a small shop where they sell fruits and vegetables. They lost all their money and assets in Baghdad, and they have received no help either from international organizations or from the Lebanese government. The only help he received came from his family who accommodated him. Here family solidarity is limited to accommodation, because political and legal constraints predominate.

These two cases clearly show that the "return" to the first country of asylum (i.e. Lebanon) is due to the difficulty or the impossibility of staying in the country of emigration (i.e. Iraq) because of insecurity, war, or discrimination. "Return" is then the only viable solution and is perceived as a temporary option. They also show that at the individual level this migration can be considered as a "return"—Palestinians originally from Lebanon going back to their first country of asylum—but if one considers the household level, it can be considered as an emigration movement towards a new country of residence, due to marriage to non-Palestinian women (i.e. Iraqi) or women coming from another part of the diaspora (i.e. Jordan).

Case Three: Emigration and Family Reunification

Kinship migratory networks has also become a very significant resource for migrants who today want to obtain legal residency in Europe, since family reunification is one of the easiest ways to settle in Europe. Certain Palestinians, who settled in Europe in the 1960s, but more especially during the 1970s, founded families in their host countries. Most of the parents I met preferred that their daughters married Muslims, and preferably Palestinians from the same camp or settlement in Lebanon. This kind of marriage is facilitated by the fact that daughters carry German, Swedish, or Danish passports. During a summer visit to Lebanon they marry and their husbands return with them to settle in Europe.

Jalal is a young refugee born in the beginning of the 1970s in a camp in the Tyre region. Because of the situation in Lebanon, he was thinking of emigrating. His uncle, who had settled in Germany in the early 1960s, had a daughter born there with German citizenship. In the summer of 1994, they came back to Lebanon and Jalal decided to marry her. She returned to Germany and arranged all the documents for him under the family reunification procedure. He obtained a one-year residency permit and found employment in the construction sector in Berlin. His experience, however, was not a happy one. His wife left him and took their daughter with her. He could not renew his residence permit, and in March 1999, he had to leave Germany and return to Lebanon. This shows the legal precariousness of the newcomers. He appealed the decision not to renew his residency permit, arguing that his daughter held German citizenship and was still living in Germany. He managed to obtain a new residency permit and went back to Germany a few months later.

It should be noted that the local effects of emigration through this channel on the country of departure are significant: family structures are deeply modified by emigration increasing gender inequalities in poor Palestinian areas. Emigrants are often young men. Therefore, in South Lebanon there are more young women then men of marriageable age. Many young Palestinian women do not get married and often remain in their parents' houses working in the agricultural sector.

Case Four: The Role of Information Flow and the Adaptation of Newcomers

Farid left Lebanon after being wounded during the 1982 Israeli invasion. He was transferred by the ICRC (Red Cross) to Cyprus and then Greece to be treated. From there, he went to East Berlin, where entry for Palestinians was easy. But he decided to go to West Germany and ask for asylum there with the help of his brother, who had already lived there. When he arrived, he found accommodation at his brother,s place and stayed there for over a year. At that time, it was forbidden for those in his situation to work and to study or to have access to social assistance. His brother, who was well integrated in the Palestinian and Arab community there, helped find him an illegal job at a restaurant sector. After a year, Farid did not get refugee status in Germany and began to think about leaving and going back to Lebanon. His family, who still resided in Lebanon, advised him to stay, and through the Palestinian refugee network, he heard that Scandinavian countries were giving refugee status to Palestinians escaping the Lebanese civil war. He decided to go to Malmö, where he asked for asylum. A few months later, he was granted refugee status and settled in Göteborg.

Farid's case is interesting because it indicates the role of the family network in facilitating the arrival of a new migrant, in the adaptation to the host society, and the diffusion of information. But it also points out the limits of kinship networks. Legal barriers in the host country remain obstacles that cannot always be circumvented.

Case Five: Kinship Network as a Financial Resource

The collection of the funds necessary to emigrate is also one of the main functions of kinship networks. The sums concerned are significant, since they represent several thousand dollars for each individual (from $4,000 to $8,000). The extended family, or even anyone from the village of origin, must pool together to gather the necessary money, which amounts to a collective loan. Once he has gathered the money, the debtor migrates and lives abroad. The only guarantee available to creditors is the membership of the migrant in a family or community network strongly structured and identified. Arriving at one's destination, the migrant refunds his debt by sending money back to his creditors. Generally, the money is sent with a relative or a friend visiting from Lebanon. The importance of the relationship between the sending community and the expatriate group is of prime importance in the operation of this system of financial solidarity. The mechanism is very efficient when the basis of the network is the family. The broader the basis is, the less the effectiveness. The case most commonly observed is the following: the father leaves to work in Germany, then, when his income allows, his elder son comes, followed by the other sons (or brothers), before the rest of the family comes, i.e., the spouse (or mother) and daughters (or sisters).

In a context of high restrictive immigration and asylum policies in the destination countries, the cost of migration is increasing and the opportunities offered to new immigrants to cross borders are very limited, especially because immigration and asylum laws are changing rapidly in European countries. Collecting money and having access to information are the two key problems for Palestinian refugees. I have observed that the most efficient networks are based on the ability of the nuclear family to collect funds as well as to obtain proper information on the destination countries in case of emigration towards Europe. The nuclear family often gives concrete help, whereas extended families give a more diffuse help. The only situation in which the extended family and village solidarity play the major role is when marriage and family reunification is used to emigrate.

Conclusion

Even if the Palestinians in Lebanon are refugees, their emigration should not be only analyzed through the forced migration schema. Palestinian migration responds not only to a multiplicity of factors that are linked to their refugee status—and can thus be considered forced—but also to a wide range of economic and social factors related to the departure and the destination countries, and can be related to a more or less voluntary process. As Nicholas Van Hear argues (2006:9–10):

> *Whichever option is chosen, what began as forced migration may transmute into other forms of movements as individuals and households decide to go or to send members abroad for family reunion, or to earn money, seek education, or search other forms of betterment. These new or mutated flows may merge with prior migratory streams of labour and trade.*

The notion of "return" (e.g. from Iraq to Lebanon) may be considered as form of "alternative return," due to the specific geopolitical situation.

A comparison of Lebanese and Palestinian emigration rates shows that both groups are strongly affected by emigration. According to the UNDP,

> *... the potential for Lebanese to emigrate remains high today, particularly in view of the prevailing economic slowdown and high unemployment. In the absence of official statistics, estimates vary and the figure of outflows of more than 100,000 persons per year in the last part of 1990s is cited as conservative.* [14]

The demographic profile of Lebanese emigrants is quite similar to the Palestinian profile and concerns mainly young males. As pointed out by the UNDP, the main reason to leave is employment. The high rate of emigration of both groups illustrates the blurring border between forced and non-forced migration. Lebanese and Palestinians suffer from economic difficulties as well as regional tensions. In this context, the position of Palestinian

---

14   *Men constituted the majority of people who migrated during this period (85 percent), and this applied to all age groups. Emigration affects more the skilled and better-educated segment of the population. Lebanese youth, who form more than one fifth of the population and almost one third of the labour force, are affected disproportionately by international migration.... The most important reason for this youth migration at present is the pursuit of economic opportunities abroad in view of high rates of youth unemployment in the country. Taken as a whole, the most frequently reported reason for migration is work (62 percent), followed by study (21 percent). Other cited reasons are joining family members abroad and marriage. (http://www.undp.org.lb)*

refugees is more precarious, discriminated against as they are by Lebanese opposition to any form of *tawtin*.[15] Emigration is not to be considered only as "forced" but also as a coping strategy in a restrictive context.

The Palestinian case in Lebanon demonstrates that a comprehensive study of refugee migration should integrate different levels of analysis as well as contextual elements. While Palestinians leave Lebanon because of legal, political, and economic forms of discrimination, they also belong to a larger movement of emigration from Lebanon that concerns the entire Lebanese society. Connections between these two emigration movements have to be explored in order to understand the possible existence of common networks. Some migratory itineraries of Palestinians migrating to Europe pass through West African countries where large Lebanese communities are settled. Palestinians also use Lebanese intermediaries to migrate both in Lebanon and in the transit countries (Doraï 2003b).

Ordinary Palestinians do not use the same kind of transnational resources (i.e., economic, juridical, or educational) as the elites. Deprived of nationality and passport, they do not enjoy the same freedom of movement. Therefore, they use transnational family and village resources that allow them to migrate. This "know-how" does not rely on economic or juridical bases but on family and village ties that cut across national borders. They use their dispersion throughout different nations as a resource. In this case, transnational resources are not only used to minimize risks and maximize benefits but to permit the international mobility of refugees, building a transnational system of solidarity.

---

15 Arabic term for "settlement" or "integration."

Bibliography

Abbas, Mahmoud. 1997. "The Housing Situation of the Palestinians in Lebanon," *Journal of Refugee Studies, Special Issue: Palestinians in Lebanon*, 10 (3):379–83.

Abu-Sitta, Salman. 2001. "The Right of Return: Sacred, Legal and Possible." In Naseer Aruri, ed., *Palestinian Refugees: The Right of Return*. London: Pluto Press.

Al-Ali, Nadje, Richard Black, and Khalid Koser. 2001. "Refugees and Transnationalism: The Experience of Bosnians and Eritreans in Europe," *Journal of Ethnic and Migration Studies*, 27 (4):615–34.

Al-Madi, Yousef. 1996. *Demographic, Economic and Social Characteristics of Palestinian Refugees in Gatherings in Lebanon: Compared study among camps*. Damascus: PCBS and UNICEF.

Al-Natour, Souheil. 1997. "The Legal Status of Palestinians in Lebanon," *Journal of Refugee Studies, Special Issue: Palestinians in Lebanon*, 10(3):360–77.

Black, Richard. 2001. "Fifty Years of Refugee Studies: From Theory to Policy," *International Migration Review*, 35:57–78.

Boyd, Monica. 1989. "Family and Personal Networks in International Migration: Recent Developments and New Agendas," *International Migration Review*, 23:638–669.

Brand, Laurie. 1988. *Palestinians in the Arab World: Institution Building and the Search for a State*. New York: Columbia University Press.

Choldin, Harvey M. 1973. "Kinship Networks in the Migration Process," *International Migration Review*, 7:163–75.

Doraï, Mohamed Kamel. 2000. "Les parcours migratoires des réfugiés vers la Suède et l'Europe du nord," *Revue d'études palestiniennes*, 75 (23):38–52.

———. 2003a. "Palestinian Emigration from Lebanon to Northern Europe: Refugees, Networks, and Transnational Practices," *Refuge*, 21 (2):23–31.

———. Mohamed Kamel. 2003b. "Les réfugiés palestiniens en Europe et en Suède. Complexité des parcours et des espaces migratoires." In M. Guillon, L. Legoux and E. Ma Mung, eds., *L'asile entre deux chaises. Droits de l'Homme et gestion des flux migratoires*, Paris: L'Harmattan, pp. 311–31.

Doraï, Mohamed Kamel and Doraï, Mohamed Larbi. 2002. "Mémoire sociale, immigration et diaspora." In Stéphane Laurens and Nicolas Roussiau, eds., *La mémoire sociale: Identité et représentations sociales*, Rennes: Presses Universitaires de Rennes, pp. 201–12.

Doraï, Mohamed Kamel, Jalal al-Husseini, and Jean-Christophe Augé. 2003. "De l'émigration au transfert? Réalités démographiques et craintes politiques en Jordanie," *Maghreb-Machrek*, 76:75–92.

Durand, Marie-Françoise. 1994. "Entre territoires et réseaux." In Bertrand Badie and Catherine Withol de Wenden, eds., *Le défi migratoire: Questions de relations internationales*. Paris: Presses de la Fondation Nationale des Sciences Politiques, pp. 141–57.

Faist, Thomas. 2000. *The Volume and Dynamics of International Migration and Transnational Social Spaces.* Oxford: Clarendon Press.

Fawcett, James T. 1989. "Networks, linkages, and migration systems," *International Migration Review*, 23:671–80.

FIDH. 2003. "Investigative International Mission, Lebanon. Palestinian Refugees: systematic discrimination and complete lack of interest on the part of the international community," Fédération Internationale des Droits de l'Homme, Report 356/2, March, p 18.

Gurak, Douglas T. and Fe Caces. 1992. "Migration Networks and the Shaping of Migration Systems." In Mary M. Kritz, Leam Lin Lean, and Hania Zlotnik, eds., *International Migration Systems: A Global Approach.* New York: Oxford University Press, pp. 150–76.

Hanafi, Sari. 2001. *Hona wa honaq: nahwa tahlil lil 'alaqa bin al-shatat al-falastini wa al markaz* (Here and There: Towards an Analysis of the Relationship between the Palestinian Diaspora and the Center). Ramallah: Muwatin and Jerusalem: Institute of Jerusalem Studies.

Hansen, Art. 1981. "Refugee Dynamics: Angolans in Zambia 1966 to 1972," *International Migration Review*, 15:175–94.

Hourani, Albert and Nadim Shehadi, eds. 1992. *The Lebanese in the World: A Century of Emigration.* London: The Centre for Lebanese Studies, I.B. Tauris & Co Ltd Publishers.

Katuszewski, Jacques and Ruwen Ogien. 1981. *Réseaux d'immigrés: Ethnographie de nulle part.* Paris: Les éditions ouvrières.

Khalidi, Walid. 1991. *Before their Diaspora: A Photographic History of the Palestinians 1876–1948.* Washington D.C.: Institute for Palestine Studies.

Koser, Khalid. 2002. "From Refugees to Transnational Communities?" In Nadje al-Ali and Khalid Koser, eds., *New Approaches to Migration? Transnational Communities and the Transformation of Home.* London and New York: Routledge, pp. 138–52.

Kritz, Mary M. and Hania Zlotnik. 1992. "Global Interactions: Migration Systems, Processes, and Policies." In Mary M. Kritz, Lin Lean Leam and Hania Zlotnik, eds., *International Migration Systems: A Global Approach.* New York: Oxford University Press, pp. 177–89.

Kunz, Egon F. 1973. "The Refugee in Flight: Kinetic Models and Forms of Displacement," *International Migration Review*, 7:125–46.

———. 1981. "Exile and Resettlement: Refugee Theory," *International Migration Review*, 15: 42–51.

Light, Ivan; Parminder Bhachu, and Stavros Karageorgis. 1993. "Migration networks and immigrant entrepreneurship." In Ivan Light, and Parminder Bhachu, eds., *Immigration and Entrepreneurship: Culture, Capital and Ethnic Networks.* New Brunswick, London: Transaction Publishers, pp. 25–49.

Loescher, Gil. 1990. "Introduction: Refugee Issues in International Relations." In Gil Loescher and Laila Monahan, eds., *Refugees in International Relations*. Oxford: Clarendon Press, pp. 1–33.

Ma Mung, Emmanuel, Doraï, Mohamed Kamel, Loyer, Frantz, Hily, Marie-Antoinette. 1998. "La circulation migratoire," *Migrations études*, 84:12.

Malkki, Liisa H. 1995. "Refugees and Exile: From 'Refugee Studies' to the National Order of Things," *Annual Review of Anthropology*, 24:495–523.

Marx, Emmanuel. 1990. "The Social World of Refugees: A Conceptual Framework," *Journal of Refugee Studies*, 3(3):189–203.

Massey, Douglas S. et al. 1988. "Theories of international migration: a review and appraisal," *Population and Development Review*, 19(3):431–466.

Montagne, Robert. 1954. "Etude sociologique de la migration des travailleurs musulmans d'Algérie en France. Cahier liminaire." In Robert Montagne, ed., *Etude sociologique de la migration des travailleurs musulmans d'Algérie en France (Cahier liminaire, cahier n° 1 à 8)*, pp. 3–33.

Radi, Lamia. 1995. "Les élites palestiniennes en Jordanie: les réseaux comme stratégie de survie." In Ariel Colonomos, ed., *Sociologie des réseaux transnationaux. Communautés, entreprises et individus: lien social et système international*. Paris: L'Harmattan, pp. 137–56.

Razqallah, Hala Nawfal. 1998. *Palestinians in Lebanon and Syria: A compared demographic study (1948–1995)*. Beirut: Dar al-Jadid (Arabic).

Richmond, Anthony H. 1994. *Global Apartheid: Refugees, Racism, and the New World Order*. Oxford: Oxford University Press.

Said, Wadie. 2001. "The Obligations of Host Countries to Refugees Under International Law: The Case of Lebanon." In Naseer Aruri, ed., *Palestinian Refugees: The Right of Return*. London, Pluto Press, pp. 123–51.

Shami, Seteney. 1993. "The Social Implications of Population Displacement and Resettlement: An Overview with a Focus on the Arab Middle East," *International Migration Review*, 101:4–33.

———. 1996. "Transnationalism and Refugee Studies: Rethinking Forced Migration and Identity in the Middle East," *Journal of Refugee Studies*, 9 (1):3–26.

Simon, Gildas. 2000. "Le concept de champ migratoire," Seminar paper for Table ronde GEOFORUM: Champs migratoires et structures urbaines, Aix-en-Provence.

Smith, Michael Peter. 2002. "Preface." In Nadje al-Ali and Khalid Koser, eds., *New Approaches to Migration? Transnational Communities and the Transformation of Home*. London: Routledge.

Tamari, Salim. 1996. *Palestinian refugee negotiations. From Madrid to Oslo II*. Washington D.C.: Institute for Palestine Studies.

Wahlbeck, Östen. 2002. "The Concept of Diaspora as an Analytical Tool in the Study of Refugee Communities," *Journal of Ethnic and Migration Studies*, 28 (2):221–38.

Van Hear, Nicholas. 2006. "Refugees in Diaspora: From Durable Solutions to Transnational Relations," *Refuge*, 23 (1):9–15.

Weiner, Myron. 1993. "Introduction: Security, Stability and International Migration." In Myron Weiner, ed., *International Migration and Security*. Boulder: Westview Press, pp. 1–35.

Zureik, Elia. 1996. *Palestinian Refugees and the Peace Process*. Washington D.C.: Institute for Palestine Studies.

Chapter 6
The Negotiation of Identity among Palestinian-American Returnee Youth

Tamara Tamimi

THE HISTORY of Palestinian migration can be traced back several genera-tions, to the time when young men traveled to North and South America and to different regions of the Middle East in search of wealth and prosper-ity for themselves and their families. While Palestinians have been coming to the U.S. since the 19th century, the two major waves of migration were in 1948 and 1967, corresponding to the Israeli occupation of Palestine and the West Bank and Gaza respectively (Aswad and Bilge 1996; Suleiman 1999).

More so than previous cohorts of Palestinian migrants to the U.S., those who arrived after 1967 maintained a strong attachment to their ethnic identity. Cainkar states about post-1967 Palestinian immigrants that, "They brought with them the customs and values of the Palestinian peasantry, at a time when the ethos of keeping Palestinian culture alive (post-1967 occupation) had gained considerable strength as a political mandate among Palestinians in the U.S. The ethos reinforces the propriety of remaining Palestinian against all odds" (1994:97). The hope of returning to Palestine guides their behavioral and social patterns in the U.S. In order to safeguard against the loss of this identity among their American-born children, parents will often send their children to live in Palestine for some time, in order to immerse them in the culture.

This paper will present the findings of qualitative fieldwork carried out in the West Bank among Palestinian children, born in the U.S. to post-1967 immigrants and who have returned to Palestine to live, some of them never having seen the country before. The objectives of the study are: 1) to explore the experiences of Palestinian-Americans in the West Bank through their narratives, 2) to review key anthropological and sociological concepts relating to migration outcomes, and 3) to apply these concepts to my preliminary findings of return outcomes among Palestinian-American youth. This study is exploratory, as no other work among Palestinian-American returnees has been published to date. Qualitative methods have been used to arrive at in-depth information from a few participants and to formulate preliminary hypotheses regarding return outcomes. Future investigations should include both quantitative and qualitative methods.

Although social scientists, demographers, political scientists, and economists have been concerned with international migration for nearly a century, return migration remains relatively unstudied. Anthropologists have paid particular attention to the conditions of globalization since the late 1980s. Studies of migration, refugees, diasporic communities, and transnationalism have offered useful theories and models in order to document and analyze the complex processes of identity formation among migrant communities but any discussion of return migration remains peripheral to these studies.

As a student of anthropology, I have always been interested in how people make migration decisions. Qualitative methods allow for an understanding of the daily life practices of individuals, including how people decide to move from one place to another, and once they have, how they maintain connections with the place they left. As a Palestinian-American who was raised with the hope of return to a land I had only visited, the narratives of these returnees resonate clearly with me and hold a special place in my heart.

Description of Fieldwork
I carried out in-depth interviews and discussion groups with a panel of 13 Palestinian-Americans, eight girls and five boys with ages ranging from 15–23, who came from the U.S. to live in the Ramallah/al-Bireh districts of the West Bank after 1993. All of them were born and raised for most of their lives in the U.S., and since their parents had lost their local residency rights, they are living in the West Bank either on Israeli-issued tourist visas or on expired visas, in violation of Israeli-imposed regulations.

Beginning with one Palestinian-American, I was able to create a "snow-ball sample" of others of the same cohort after I asked her to create a list of all the returnees she knew. I combined interviews and discussion groups. The interviews were semi-structured, guided by open-ended questions, which allowed for interviewees to present a narrative of nearly two hours each. The discussion groups were structured the same way, allowing for maximum interaction between participants, rather than between the participants and myself. In the end, I conducted four one-on-one tape-recorded interviews and two tape-recorded discussion groups with six participants in each.

Two of the one-on-one interviews took place at my home, where I invited them for tea and coffee. The other two took place at Birzeit University, one in an empty classroom, and the other outside in a courtyard where the students have lunch. Both of the discussion groups took place in Birzeit University's computer room, where the "English-speaking" students spent their free time.

The presence of Palestinian-Americans could be seen and felt on the streets of Ramallah when I was there in 1998, especially in the town's central area where people come to shop, work or spend time in the many restaurants and cafes. Palestinian-American youth, dressed in their urban style baggy jeans and over-sized sweatshirts, could be heard speaking English mixed with Arabic euphemisms, gathered at any one of the new American style restaurants that had opened there.

The parents of the returnee youth I interviewed in Ramallah were part of a post-1967 wave of Palestinian immigrants to the U.S. who were for the most part, raised with this ethos which emphasizes the importance of maintaining the Palestinian ethnic and national identity while in diaspora. They come from San Francisco, Chicago and its surrounding suburbs, and the U.S. Virgin Islands. Their average age at the time of the interviews was 20 years, all of them having been in the West Bank since high school.

I asked the participants questions that resulted in descriptive information about their lives in the U.S. including their neighborhoods, leisure activities, community and friends. Most of them lived in suburban neighborhoods, among "white" people or people of other ethnic groups. Only a few lived within Arab communities and had Arab friends. While I did not ask questions to arrive at socioeconomic status indicators, I did get the general sense that most of the interviewees were of the lower middle class judging from the description of their neighborhoods and the type of activities they engaged in while in the U.S., placing them in the same socio-economic position as the cohort of post-1967 immigrants in Chicago described by Cainkar (1994).

Life in the West Bank

The signing of the Oslo peace accord in 1993 marked the beginning of a major influx of Palestinian exiles to the West Bank and Gaza. This movement occurred despite the fact that the Israeli government denies the majority of Palestinian exiles the right to return to live in Israel, the West Bank, or Gaza. Estimates of the number of post-Oslo returnees range between 40,000 and 100,000 (Sayre and Olmsted 1999:2). With such a wide range, it is clear that there are no accurate immigration estimates kept by the Palestinian Authority. According to the Palestinian Central Bureau of Statistics (PCBS), the total number of people born outside the Palestinian National Authority (PNA) territories who lived there in 1997 was 250,697. Nearly ten percent of them (24,542) were living in the Ramallah/al-Bireh districts, second only to Gaza (PCBS 2002).

The most prominent group of these returnees are officials of the PLO and their families who were based in Tunisia and who were allowed into the territories to staff the Palestinian National Authority, predominately in Gaza. The second largest group of post-Oslo returnees are from the U.S. These are families and individuals who had left to escape the pressures of military occupation, and who have returned after the withdrawal of Israeli troops from those regions of the West Bank and Gaza where the PNA held limited control. The PCBS does not have records indicating the number of these returnees, but out of the 250,697 foreign born Palestinians residing in the PNA territories in 1999, 7300 of them were born in the U.S. Of these, 83 percent of them were age 19 and younger (Abunimah from PCBS figures, personal communication, 2003.

The returnees I interviewed lived in the villages surrounding Ramallah, Birzeit, Jerusalem, and Bethlehem including Yabrood, Ein Senia, Deir Dubwan, Surda, Betunia, Beit Sureek, Beit Hanina, and Bateer (see Table 1). These are all the home villages of their parents. At some point during their adolescence, these young people were sent with their mothers to live in the West Bank, while their fathers stayed in the U.S. The residents of most villages throughout the West Bank are kin from the same *hamula* (clan). Since endogamous marriage was and continues to be practiced among Palestinians, the village to which they return is home to both mother and father. With extremely cohesive relationships, few nuclear families live alone within a household. Families typically share homes of several floors and prepare and eat meals together. The entire village can be characterized as an extended family and also as a unit of social control.

Table 1: **Returnee Profile**

	Name	Sex	Age	Origin	Residence in Palestine
1	Rana	Female	21	San Francisco, CA	Yabrood
2	Alaa	Male	20	Chicago, IL	Ein Senia
3	Amal	Female	21	Midwest, small town	Deir Dubwan
4	Leila★	Female	20	U.S. Virgin Islands	Bateer
5	Lana★	Female	22	U.S. Virgin Islands	Bateer
6	Sina★	Female	20	U.S. Virgin Islands	Bateer
7	Reem	Female	23	San Francisco, CA	Surda
8	Ramzi	Male	20	San Francisco, CA	Ramallah
9	Mustafa	Male	21	Chicago, IL	Betunia
10	Maha	Female	19	Chicago, IL	Betunia
11	Rami★★	Male	15	Chicago, IL	Beit Sureek
12	Jamil★★	Male	20	Chicago, IL	Beit Sureek
13	Salwa	Female	20	Libertyville, IL	Beit Hanina

★ Sisters
★★ Brothers

I asked several of the interviewees to tell me about the villages in which they live. When discussing the village of Surda, Reem told me that the residents are from two big families. She goes on to describe the village:

> It is just generally a neighborhood on a hill. The whole thing is just two streets, but they are long streets. There are stores, there are supermarkets, they are actually coming up in the world. There are dukans [small corner store], there is a billiard hall, newly built for the shebab [young men] in the village.
>
> So that is it, really. Very homey. It is quaint. You can go around the whole village in like 20 minutes, so it is really quaint. And most of the time, that is what I and my friends also do, we just stroll, you know just walk around; we walk around for like an hour or two, and then go back home.

Houses and cars are used by returnees in various international contexts as displays of their success abroad (King 2000; Gmelch 1992). The "villas" built by Palestinian returnees are an example. Reem explained that in Surda, "People are starting to come back from the U.S. and starting to build their houses now. A lot of old style houses that have been built on top of them. Old style houses that they leave like that, but newer inside."

For the most part, returnee youth find life in the village constricting and boring. This is especially true for the boys who are accustomed to coming and going as they please in the U.S., with a comparatively larger selection of recreational activities. I asked Alaa during the discussion group, if he enjoyed living in Palestine:

> **Alaa:** *If you had some of the facilities that they have in the U.S. here, then yeah, this would be like paradise.*

> **Q:** *Like what kind of facilities?*

> **Alaa:** *Commercial, educational, recreational, anything. Because you know, when a person here is bored he has nothing to do.*

> **Reem interjects:** *Walk around in the neighborhood.*

> **Alaa:** *Exactly, or talk about people, or just look at girls and start making comments. When a person in the U.S. is bored, he would go to a movie, go to a ball game or something.*

The boys also complained more than the girls about the lack of systems and rules within Palestinian society. Comparing the U.S. to Ramallah, Mustafa explained, "Life is easier in the U.S., but this is our country, so…" I asked how life in the U.S. was easier, and he continued:

> *Being alone. There are no rules or regulations—no one to bother you. For example, the other day I went to pick up my wife's identification card from the municipality. Nobody respects the others. When you are in line, they just walk right in front of you. You do not see that happen in the U.S. If you see a line, you follow it.*

Results of the Qualitative Study

This study offers a preliminary look into the lives of Palestinian-American returnee youth in the West Bank. The sample size was small enough to allow for in-depth discussions on several key issues, but not large enough to make any broad generalizations. There are however, six major themes that dominate the returnees' narratives upon which I base my hypotheses to be discussed in the next section.

Restrictions in the U.S. The first of these themes concerns life in U.S. for the returnees and the restrictions on their behavior that were placed on them by their families.

> **Rana:** *Well, over there my parents were strict. You know, they are Arab. My parents would let me go out but not at night. The boyfriend-girlfriend thing was out of the question. Talking to guys on the phone, going to guys' houses, having guys come over was all out of question. Going out with guys was also out of question. They knew we knew boys from school and stuff, but that was all.*

> **Alaa:** *Yeah, like me personally. I would not talk to girls on the phone, nor would they come to the house. But my mother knew that I knew girls from school—classmates—and there was nothing wrong with that so long as it was held within limits.*

> **Salwa:** *A lot of the Palestinians I knew did not even teach their children Arabic because they thought that they were coming to a better world. They taught them certain values, like caring about education and stuff like that. They had rules, like they could date, but they were not allowed to have sex before marriage. So they were really liberal.*

Palestinian-American youth often avoid friendships with non-Arabs because of the difficulty in explaining their families' rules and why they cannot do the same things that their peers can.

> **Rana:** *Given that my parents were strict, I got tired of giving my friends excuses for not being able to go out. I figured, here with my own people, they all feel the same way I feel. It would be a lot easier for me if I decided to come and live here. My mom, sisters, and brothers followed a year after.*

> **Reem:** *Well, my best friend was an Arab. She was a Jordanian, and I hung out with her most of the time. Her friends, whom I got to know through her, were Palestinian. Basically, those were my*

in-crowd. I did have friends outside the Palestinian-Arab community, but I did not really do much with them.

Q: *How come?*

Reem: *Because a lot of times they would want to do things that I just could not do. Like, go out of the city to some place else, Santa Cruz where you had to sleep over, but my parents would not let me sleep over any place. Go to parties that did not start till 10 or 11 o'clock, which was the time I would have to be home. I also could not go to their houses a lot. My parents would say that I was over-doing it or, "no, it is better not." I mean, that is why I basically stayed with the Arabs, because Arabs are more understanding since they had to go through the same things, and we all just had to have as much fun as we could.*

Palestinians of the post-1967 immigration wave to the U.S. do their best to pass on their Palestinian national and cultural identity to their American-born children. For these parents, the U.S. is full of dangers and threats to their attempts to do so, which become especially apparent once their children reach adolescence. These dangers include threats to the respect and dignity of their families, to the physical safety of their children, and to the preservation of their identity as Palestinians.

The importance of the cultural value of sexual morality and how it relates to the behavior of girls and women within Palestinian families in the U.S. has been discussed earlier. For many Palestinian parents, the fact that dating and premarital sex are widely accepted in American society and that their daughters are exposed to such values on a daily basis poses a consistent threat to the standing of the entire family within the community. Revealing dress styles among American teenagers, and the popular habit of sleeping over-night at a friend's house are also unacceptable to many Palestinian parents and present a conflict between them and their teenage daughters. The honor of the family is judged by their reference group within the community, and rests primarily on the behavior of women. For this reason, gossip serves as an important tool for social control.

Perhaps the major underlying fear among Palestinians in the U.S. is the loss of their identity as Palestinians, including the loss of Islam and its values and the loss of the Arabic language. While most immigrants strive to retain at least some aspects of their traditional culture and values, many Palestinians in the U.S. feel that doing so is a matter of survival, especially as their land, identity, and political existence are threatened by Israeli military occupation. Parents of American-born youth fear that through socializing with non-Arabs and through intermarriage their children will lose sense of their Palestinian identity.

Against all of the above threats, Palestinian parents in the U.S. employ a number of methods to protect their children. These include the teaching of Islamic values, which include the prohibition of alcohol, drugs, and premarital sex, and the sanctity of sexual modesty for men and women. Parents also attempt to control their children's behavior through strict rules within the family with various forms of punishment if broken. These rules often relate to the dress and conduct of their female children.

America as dangerous. A second and related theme discussed by the returnees is their parents' perceptions of the hazards of raising children in America—hazards they hope to avoid by sending them to live in Palestine.

> **Salwa:** *I sort of went from being an achiever, over excelling, and wanting to go to Harvard to wearing black, piercing my ears, shaving my head, and stuff like that. So my parents went a little crazy because I started hanging out with the wrong group for a while. They brought me here to sort of, balance it out. They think that I would get calmer and that there would be less peer pressure.*

> **Ramzi:** *I would say a lot of them came back because they had got into trouble in the U.S. I know people who are here because they are wanted by the police. I know one guy who was in my class and came here because he was a suspect in a drive-by shooting. There was a man killed and they did not know if it was his gun that shot him or the guy he was with. He was from Houston. Some people come here because they robbed others. Some people come because they want their kids to know the culture and stuff. But a lot of guys are here because of the problems they have in the U.S., drugs and things like that. The girls too, some of them come because of problems they had with guys.*

> **Rana:** *My parents said that I would rather have Arab friends than American friends. They would always say that you could not trust Americans.*

Lana: *There, my father was really strict with us. Over here, we can go and come as we want, we have a car, and we go out and things like that.*

Q: *Is that because your father is not here?*

Lana: *No, it is because he allows us. Even though he is not here, he knows what we are doing. He trusts us over here more than over there.*

Sina: *There, they say that they do not trust the people. Everybody is like us over here, so we go out together. Over there, we could not do that, because people would talk and because my father would not let us to go out. The people there are American and my father would not want us to get involved with them.*

With adolescence often comes conflict between parents and their children, when the values of the family are suddenly challenged by those the children learn outside home. Palestinian parents often send their American-born children to live in Palestine during their teenage years, in order to remove them from what is seen as a dangerous environment and to immerse them in the Palestinian culture. In the most typical scenario, fathers will stay in the U.S. to continue working or run the family business, while the mother and children go to Palestine to live within the home village of the father and/or mother. While the children may be familiar with the West Bank from periodic visits, they are often unaware of their parents' plan to relocate them. Many of the returnees I interviewed met this news with much anger and resentment:

Salwa: *I was not told that I was going to stay here.*

Q: *Oh, you weren't?*

Salwa: *No. I was told that I was coming here for two weeks.*

Q: *And then?*

Salwa: *And then they were just like "we're staying here." It was like a shock. I just went crazy. I felt like "you cannot do that to me; I just thought we were coming here for a visit."*

Q: *Had you been here before?*

Salwa: *I came here for visits, but that was about it. And it was just like "you cannot keep me here." You know? It is a culture that I do not know; it is a place I do not know; it is a place I do not want to be in right now. They would not let me go back. So that is when I rebelled. Even when I graduated with honors, they still would not let me go back. I do not know what they want from me. It is really hard.*

Reem also had a difficult time accepting her new home:

Reem: *I hated coming here for visits. In 1992, I knew that in a year's time we would come back to stay, and I was really in a bad mood about it. The last time we were here was the worst. I went crazy on my parents and everything. "I do not want to come back here." I knew what I was in store for, I knew what this country had to offer and it was not what I wanted. So, when I finally came here, I actually went on strike. I stayed in my house for nine whole months not going anywhere.*

Since 1994, Palestinian-Americans have increasingly become a visible and discernable subgroup of Ramallah's populace. They are easily distinguishable from non-returnees by way of their language and dress, the places they choose to frequent, and ways in which they socialize. American-English is often heard in the streets in downtown Ramallah and in restaurants like the American hamburger chain "Checkers" or cafes like "Kan Bata Zaman" where Palestinian-Americans come to meet friends and socialize. Soon after the end of the first *intifada* and the arrival of the Palestinian Authority, new restaurants, cafes, bars, pool halls, and dance clubs were opened and continue to be frequented by returnees and locals alike.

Three Palestinian commercial radio stations also opened soon after, "The Voice of Love and Peace," "Menara," and "Amwaj." All three stations broadcast English-language music shows hosted by Palestinian-Americans. In November 1998, *Ha'aretz Magazine* featured an article titled "Radio Ramallah." Referring to these English language programs, the article states:

These programs have built an on-air home for Palestinians reared in the U.S. and displaced halfway through high school to the newly Palestinian controlled West Bank. They have also introduced

Palestinians who have never left the West Bank to American-style song, dance, talk shows, targeted advertising and their attendant radically new values.

During call-in shows, Palestinian-Americans can be heard dedicating songs to their friends and often voicing problems that they face adjusting to life in Palestine. English language shows and the young people who call in have also influenced the conversational styles and musical tastes of local residents who may have never left the West Bank. "What's up" has become a typical Ramallah greeting.

One of the most interesting ways through which Palestinian-Americans mark their presence in Ramallah is the graffiti I found in 1998, which is similar to that found on the sides of buildings in American inner cities. This graffiti replaced the spray painted political slogans that remained from the days of the *intifada*. Palestinian-Americans, many of whom have come from urban centers of the U.S., place visible markers of their presence in Ramallah using English nicknames or "tags" that reflect not any kind of gang activity but merely their presence as individuals and as a subgroup of Ramallah's populace.

Palestinian-American returnee youth often express their identity in ways that emphasize their "American-ness" and their difference. This is especially true shortly after their arrival, when they have yet to adjust and integrate into West Bank life and society. Salwa described how she and her friends resisted assimilation:

> *I think for a long time since we were here we used to go to Jaffa Road [in West Jerusalem] all the time, and even McDonalds. We would not eat any food here but we would go to McDonalds and gorge. A lot of my American friends would only wear American clothes—we would never buy any clothes here. We would not eat falafel or any food like that. We would never go shopping in Ramallah. We kept the American culture alive through music and TV shows—not watching Arabic TV shows, not speaking Arabic.*

Ramallah has at least four high schools with English tracks to accommodate returnees from the U.S. According to Salwa, the students in each school had particular characteristics. The returnees at Friends School are considered the rich, smart kids who come from middle or upper middle class neighborhoods in the U.S. Students at al-Urduniyeh and at al-Jinan are said to come from the urban centers of American cities. These young people affiliate with Mexican-American and African-American youth cultures in particular, and bring to Ramallah the language, dress, and attitudes of these cultures. Being clearly different from the returnees of the upper middle class and from the larger local society, this group is perceived in a negative was by the latter two. Salwa related how her parents took her sister out of al-Jinan School. After their daughter had begun to change her dress and hairstyle, her parents became worried that "instead of becoming more Palestinian, she is becoming Mexican." Even though the daughters were raised in a suburban environment, Salwa's sister, like other young people, found the urban youth culture appealing and imitated how her peers at school dressed and behaved.

Gossip. Several of the Palestinian-American girls I interviewed spoke about gossip within their communities both in the U.S. and in Palestine.

> **Rana:** *Well, my parents are somewhat religious, they both pray, and we fasted for as long as I can remember. I mean, they tried their best. Maybe they should have tried harder, but they tried. However, usually what they did is that they would tell us what to do without telling us why we should do it, and their main reason was that people would talk. If you are going to listen to that, it is only going to be for a certain period of time, because you tend to get tired worrying about what people say. So, I guess we would not know it is against our religion, we would know that it is against other people's standards. For example, I would not think about having a boyfriend not because it is against our religion, but because I would be afraid of what people would say. I see that a lot, I do it too. I do things that are proscribed, but I am not afraid of the punishment I would get in the future, I am only afraid if somebody saw me and talk about me. It should not be that way.*

> **Lana:** *Everybody is like us over here, so we go out together. Over there, we could not do that because people would talk and because my father would not let us to go out.*

> **Reem:** *It was fun hanging around with your friends, going to places, walking around, not having to worry about people or be careful with what you are doing. Over there, you are just free to do what you want to do. You do not have to worry. Your parents do not say that you cannot go out, or fear what people will say. In the U.S., people do not*

know you and do not care; and even if they did know you, they still would not care.

Reem's experience in the U.S. varies from the other participants in that she found life in Palestine more constricting than the U.S. Her quote reveals that her family was more concerned about gossip among their community in Palestine than they were while in the U.S. and, therefore, placed tighter restrictions on her behavior once she moved there. As a result, Reem was one of the few females I interviewed who was very unhappy living in Palestine. Gossip is used as a mechanism for social control among Palestinians in the U.S. and in Palestine.

Parents may attempt to control their children's behavior through the threat of gossip. Having a reputation can be devastating for a young woman and for her family. The worst wrongdoings involve dating, drinking, premarital sex, or dress and public behavior that can lead to rumors of involvement in such activities. Even though the returnees I interviewed are quite conservative and religious, they complained frequently about being the subject of gossip which, like in the U.S., serves to control people's behavior in public. Rana told me that she "carries herself differently," and that in Palestine she's "more careful and laughs less in public."

Personal freedom. The issue of "freedom" is an important one for the youth I interviewed. Questions that asked them to compare their lives in the U.S. to their lives in Palestine inevitably resulted in a discussion about freedom.

Q: *What do your parents think about you going out here?*

Reem: *I know if my dad were here, I would not be going out as much.*

Q: *Where is your dad?*

Reem: *He is in the States, back in San Francisco. I know if he were here, I would not go out as much. He would say, "What would people say? No, no we do not want people to see you going and coming. What do you need to go there for? What do you need to come here for?" all that stuff. My mother is more relaxed about things like that, and anyway, she is used to it. Besides, most of the time, she is not home to see me whether or not I am there.*

> **Leila:** *I had a lot more freedom when I first came. I did not really have much freedom in the U.S. because we could not do much where we were, just go to school and back home. Just hanging out. But here, there is more. It is much better.*

> **Amal:** *I think I have more freedom. When I came here, I started to have more freedom because my mom felt no harm if guys called me from work when they needed something, and if I talked to guys at Birzeit. Seriously, it seems like having more freedom here, but it is in a different shape and form.*

> **Rana:** *Many parents think that it is safer here and that they can trust people more.*

Such comments suggest that moving to Palestine has afforded some returnees the ability to come and go as they please with less interference from their parents. Some families become less concerned with the comings and goings of their children because of the fact that the local social environment reinforces the same values they are teaching at home. The dangers that threatened the family in the U.S. are no longer present. Also, the unit of social control is no longer limited to the household and immediate family as it is in the U.S., but is often widened to include the extended family living in the same village who closely monitor the behavior of their male and, especially, female relatives in public.

Religion. The returnees I interviewed had been in Ramallah for at least two years, most of them longer. They had graduated from high school and were attending university at the time of the interviews. By the time I spoke to them, they had had a chance to adjust to life in the West Bank and to reflect on the experience of return. Boys usually have the option of going back to the U.S. to attend university. The fact that those I met had not done so may mean that they were content with staying in the West Bank.

The move from the U.S. to the West Bank has certainly changed these returnees and how they felt about their identities. For example, most of the young people I interviewed became more religious after moving to Palestine. Being all Muslim, many began to adhere more strictly to Islamic codes of conduct including praying, fasting, and for women, wearing the headscarves or *hijab* (veil).

When I asked during a discussion group if they were religious, Jamil responded:

I started when I came here. My mother is Christian and my father is a Palestinian Muslim, but he is not religious. After I came here, I learned six or seven Quranic suras. Before that, I had not known anything. Now I also know how to pray. My brother does not speak Arabic but he can read any sura from the Quran, thank God, and I am very proud of that because we are not a religious family.

I asked Mustafa if they were as religious before going back to Palestine, and he responded:

No, I did not know anything about this. I knew very little. Although my mom taught me religion, but it did not hit me until I came here.

Rana explained why she had recently decided to wear the *hijab*:

I guess the more time you spend here and the more you see people around you wearing it, you kind of learn to appreciate why they wear it. Do you know what I mean?

When I asked why religion is important to her, Maha explained:

It makes you feel like you are doing something right. You know what this right thing is, so why not do it? Why not follow the straight path? Like I said, life is not about having fun. At this point in my life, you have to know where you stand, you have to know who you are. I mean, okay, we came here and we found this part of ourselves, being Palestinian, our culture and everything, but aside from that Islam is a whole different story. Religion in general should be a major part of a person.

Negative perception of returnees by the local population. All of the returnees I interviewed agreed that the perception of them held by the local population in the West Bank is essentially a negative one.

Leila: *It seems like at Birzeit they do not really like us that much.*

Q: *What do you mean?*

Leila: *Because the other day a teacher was talking to the students about English-speaking, about how they are all conceited, and how* *they do not like the local Arabs, and all the students were agreeing with him. "That is true, they are conceited and they do not like us, they do not socialize with us, they do not talk to us."*

Rana: *Well, in the beginning when you come everything is fine and you do what you want as long as you are not doing anything wrong to yourself or harming your reputation in any way. But then, when the people here see you have come from the U.S., they tend to think negatively of you and assume many things about you. For example, when you go to a restaurant, people in the village find it unacceptable. You try to do many things so as not to get people talk about you, and you end up confused.*

Sina: *They do not believe us if we say we have not done anything; the automatic assumption is that we have seen and done everything. We are tired of it.*

Alaa: *People think this way because when they go to the U.S., they do whatever they want.*

Salwa: *I think I might have liked the U.S. better. I really cannot say. In the future, if I find a good profession here, I would not mind doing something for this country. After the* intifada *and all the problems the Palestinians have been facing, they need help. But on the other hand some of them are so ignorant when it comes to Palestinian-Americans that I just get aggravated and think I am never coming here again. It is like this paradox.*

Q: *Can you talk about this conflict?*

Salwa: *I try to convince myself that the uneducated think that all Americans are this way and that way. They are really negative when it comes to Palestinian-Americans. They think we are snobby, but they just do not understand the culture. If I hang out with liberal people, they are okay. But the comments you hear on the street get really aggravating, like the automatic assumption that Palestinian-Americans date and drink and do this and that, when, it is not true. If they look at their own culture, there are a lot of Palestinians themselves who date and do whatever they like. It is aggravating at times.*

In fact, Palestinian-American returnees are under close scrutiny by the local residents which is partly due to their perceptions of them as holding lower moral standards than those who had never lived in the U.S. Comparably, Ruth Mandel describes the experiences of adolescent second-generation Turkish immigrants to Germany who, after returning to Turkey to live, have a particularly difficult time adapting. She states, "Older girls often complain of being ostracized, since their peers assume they are not virgins by virtue of their connections with Germany—a land associated with infidels, immorality and promiscuity" (1990:162). While Palestinian residents are not necessarily as conservative in their perceptions of Palestinian-Americans, there is a degree of tension in the relationship between the local population and the returnees. This was especially true in the mid 1990s when a large number of Palestinians from the U.S. came to live in cities like Ramallah and its surrounding villages.

In fact, the youth I interviewed believe that returnees from the U.S. are more conservative than the local youth. When we discussed the negative perceptions of them, Lana said: "They do not understand that our parents are very strict with us. You would be surprised. We hold onto our traditions more than they do here." Alaa added, "That is true. Ninety percent of the girls who come back pray and fast. The majority of the girls, of the people here, do not."

Nevertheless, returnees feel that they are "put under a microscope" which makes them feel like "animals in a zoo." According to my interviewees, the two most prevalent perceptions of returnees can be summarized in the Arabic words *say'een* and *sheb'aneen*. The root word *saye'* broadly means, "gone astray." It is used to describe those who have nothing to do but wander around misbehaving and breaking social norms. The root word *shab'an* literally means full (with food). The closest translation in English would be "decadent." The implication is that the returnees have been spoiled in the U.S. Those I interviewed believe that the general perception of them by locals is that they are "arrogant," "spoiled," "conceited," and "snobby." When used with the expression *saye', shab'an* has the added implication that returnees have taken part in activities that are morally unacceptable, like premarital sex and drinking alcohol.

Regardless of the unwelcomed reception many returnees may have experienced, most of the ones I met were friends both with other returnees and with the local population. In high school, returnees are separated physically and socially from the rest of the students because of the special classes they take through the English language tracks. The returnees I interviewed did continue to socialize together as a group, but they also related well to others perhaps because of the amount of time they have had since their immigration to adjust and meet people, and because of the experience of going to university where they take classes with Arabic-speaking students.

There are fundamental differences between the way boys and girls experience return. This is mainly because the restrictions on behavior and movement that are imposed on youth by their parents, families, and communities fall predominantly on females. Also, boys may have internalized many of the values taught to them by their families and communities, values that often afford them social power by virtue of their gender.

None of the male Palestinian-American returnees I interviewed complained about restrictions on their movement or conduct. In fact, all were quite complacent about being in Palestine. The complaints they did have were very different than those of the girls. When I asked the boys what it was about Palestine they did not like, they brought up issues relating to the lack of social organization and systems, the lack of facilities, and of boredom. The fact that young male returnees have far less restrictions placed on them by their families, and by society as a whole, and the fact that after high school, many are given the opportunity to return to the U.S. to study while girls are generally not, makes the entire experience of living in Palestine very different for them.

Nevertheless, the males and females I interviewed still seemed to form a cohesive social group, united by their shared identity, their shared longing for that which they miss in the U.S., and by the reality that they remain different than the larger populations around them—both in Palestine and in the U.S.

Causes and Outcomes of Return among Palestinian-Americans

It is difficult to make broad generalizations about the causes and outcomes of return migration with so little empirical evidence. Nevertheless, the literature does highlight economic, social, and family related reasons as the main causes for return among first-generation immigrants, with pull factors having much more influence over the return decision than push factors. King has classified the predominant cause and effect factors of return as economic, social, family/life cycle, and political (2000:14).

There has been a very limited amount of work done to document the causes of return among Palestinian immigrants to the U.S. specifically. A study conducted by Cainkar (1998) among Palestinians in Chicago revealed that many would prefer to return than to stay in the U.S. The stated reasons for this preference related to the quality of social relations in the U.S. as compared to the West Bank, and to the perceived hazards of raising children in the U.S.

The pilot to a follow-up study conducted among Palestinian immigrants from Jordan has shown that if resources permit, Palestinians would prefer to live a transnational existence between the U.S. and Jordan, where movement between the two would be timed according to particular stages in the family's life cycle (Cainkar et al. 2004). Children's adolescence and the adults' old age are the two stages in the life cycle when return is most likely. This finding can be corroborated by my own research and personal experience. Cainkar and her colleagues explain that Palestinian immigrants from Jordan living in Chicago worry about their children's exposure to risks, such as gangs and drugs, while they struggle to ingrain in them an appreciation of their cultural and religious heritage. Such difficulties are exacerbated during their children's adolescence and, therefore, many prefer to return to Jordan during this stage of their family's life cycle. Adult immigrants over the age of 60 find that after their working years are over, they prefer to return to the social relationships, which they left behind in search of economic gain. These social relationships are an important form of social capital for the elderly.

In reference to King's diagram of causes and effects of return migration (2000:14), the main causal factors for Palestinians are those labeled "family/life cycle" and "social" where kinship and social ties, nostalgia and racism found in the host country all pull immigrants to their home countries. Another key causal factor for Palestinians is the socialization and protection of their American-born children.

The literature also points to the difficulties faced by first-generation returnees in their attempts to re-integrate. When discussing the possible outcomes of return migration, King refers to the "dual hypothesis" which posits that in urban to rural return migration, "the more urban and industrial the value structure of the returning migrant, the greater will be the conflict in re-adaptation, and the greater will be the probability of the returnee inducing social change" (2000:19). The opposite is also true, where the more traditional the values held by the returnee, the less trouble s/he will have in readjusting and the less likely that social change will be induced.

A few theorists have also developed models to help determine the probability of return migration among first-generation immigrants from specific ethnic communities (Massey 1987; Beenstock 1993; Licht and Steiner 1993). However, little work has been done on the return outcomes among second-generation immigrant children (even though the phenomenon of "return" among this population is common across ethnic groups).

As was shown to be true for assimilation outcomes, outcomes of return migration vary depending on the interplay of key variables. I will discuss some of the possible outcomes of return for Palestinian-American youth, including a discussion of what the key variables for this cohort may be.

The importance of the "dual hypothesis" lies in the implicit generalization that the more similar the value structure of the returnee to the community, the easier the return process will be, and vice versa. Among the second-generation Palestinian returnees I interviewed, it was those who shared the value system of their parents and of the community who seemed to have the least trouble adjusting to life in the West Bank.

This point is exemplified through a comparison of responses from two of my interviewees, Maha and Reem. Compared to the rest of the respondents, Maha seemed the best adjusted and the most content to be living in Palestine. When I asked her about her life in the U.S., she responded, "What do you mean? Like freedom? When I was there I was free to do whatever I wanted, and here it's the same thing. My parents respect me and respect my views, so I am free to do whatever I want." When we discussed the issue of dating she stated, "If an Arab girl wanted to have a boyfriend it would be secret, but to me, I did not bother because I really did not care about those kinds of things."

Reem, on the other hand, told me that while in the U.S., she did have boyfriends. When I asked if she ever did things without her parents' consent she said:

> I would say that I am with Patricia, my best friend, who is an Arab. I would say I am going out with her, and most likely we would be double-dating. But most of the time if I had a boyfriend it would be from school, so if I cannot see him outside school I would see him in school. There would be my aunt. She would help me out. There was one time when I really wanted to go to Homecoming, and I snuck out. I pretended like I was going to bed early and I snuck out and they found out about that one.

Maha was very clear about her religious convictions. When I asked her what role religion plays in her life she responded:

> A big role in my life. I am Muslim, and I pray, and hopefully I will be wearing the headscarf soon because it is right. If you really look into what the Quran says, you would know that it is right.

When I asked Reem the same question she responded:

> *Personally, not a big part. I have religion in my life but it does not play a major role. It does not always dictate what I do. But I do believe in God, and the powers that be. I do not go to Jerusalem and pray in the mosque. I do not wear a headscarf. My dad prays, fasts, and is very religious. My grandfather, all my family, the older generation, they are religious and they pray.*

> **Q:** *Has your family ever said that they want religion to play a larger role in your life?*

> **Reem:** *My father, yeah.*

> **Q:** *So has he ever asked you maybe to wear the* hijab*?*

> **Reem:** *He has asked me, yeah. But he also knows that he cannot force me now that I am this old.*

I asked Maha how she felt about living in Palestine. She answered, "I am happy here, I am satisfied. When I first came here it was difficult to adjust to society and its ways, and the culture because I was not used to it. But now I am happy, and do not want anything more. I go to college." When I asked her if she had been back to the U.S. she replied, "I have not been back. My parents gave me the chance to. I mean they told me if I wanted to go back and study in the States it was fine, but I chose to stay here because I thought it would be a good experience."

Of all the respondents, Reem was perhaps the most discontented to be in Palestine. She is the one who said that she did not leave her house for nine months after she was forced to move to the West Bank. When I asked her if she planned on moving back to the U.S. she said, "Yes. When the time is right. I do not plan on living here for the rest of my life."

Language can also be key variable in determining the outcome of return. Reem for example, spoke very basic Arabic and subsequently had serious difficulties socializing with local Palestinians.

> **Reem:** *I feel very awkward to hang out with anyone who is born and raised here.*

> **Q:** *How come?*

Reem: *Maybe because of the language.*

Q: *What are your Arabic skills like?*

Reem: *My spoken Arabic is very basic. In addition, sometimes I feel like even if I was able to communicate with people here, I do not know what to talk about because I do not feel like we really have very much in common. Neither the girls nor the boys. So I am always more reserved when I am with the locals here. With Palestinian-Americans you can act as you wish, you can be silly, and they do not care. You just let loose with them and you tighten up when you are with the locals here.*

Maha clearly had less conflict between her own values and those of her parents and of the larger West Bank community than did Reem. It is also clear that Maha is better adjusted and more content to be in Palestine, an indication of the validity of hypotheses that claim the closer the value system of the returnee and his/her immediate social environment, the easier the adjustment process.

In addition to congruence in value systems and working knowledge of Arabic, returnee youth were better able to adjust to life in the West Bank if they had lived within a community of Arabs in the U.S. This is especially true if they had internalized the key values and normative expectations of their parents' culture. Visits to the West Bank prior to return also help ease the "cultural shock" for young people, especially if visits were long enough to allow them to adjust and to establish relationships.

The experiences they have while in the West Bank also have an effect on the outcome of return for Palestinian-Americans. Generally, village life is more difficult to adjust to for these young people than the more cosmopolitan settings of Ramallah or Jerusalem. Young returnees from the U.S. find the slow pace of village life boring and the tight social and familial relations constricting. However, most of the young women I spoke to experienced a greater degree of freedom in Palestine, which made the experience of living there a positive one. Conversely, those who felt they had more freedom in the U.S. were discontented and hoped to go back there. Finally, the negative reception of the returnees by the local population hindered the adjustment process for these young people, who felt that they were being judged unfairly. Nevertheless, such negative perceptions did not dissuade them from forming relationships with locals over time.

Summation

This study has offered preliminary findings related to the experiences of Palestinian-American youth who have returned to live in Palestine, a topic that has so far gone unstudied. Because of the lack of information available on these migrants, qualitative methods have been used in order to arrive at key themes through in-depth interviews and discussion groups. These preliminary findings relating to the experiences of Palestinian-American returnees should be explored further through a larger scale study, including quantitative methods, in order to test key variables.

The findings of this study include factors that may be associated with positive return outcomes for Palestinian-American youth. The assessment of a migration outcome can be measured in several ways, including assimilation results. Some of the factors that can be associated with assimilation in this case are language knowledge and preferences, ethnic identity and self-esteem (see Portes and Rumbaut 2001). In cases of return migration, a successful outcome may be defined as successful re-integration. In the case of Palestinian-American returnee youth, there are a few additional variables that should be tested further for their impact on return outcomes. These include congruence in value systems between parents and children prior visits to Palestine, place of residence in Palestine, sense of personal freedom and the reception by the local community. If these factors are indeed significantly associated with return outcomes for Palestinian-American youth, their relationship to other return populations should also be tested.

Today's immigration has become increasingly transnational, where people maintain connections to and identifications with more than one country or nation-state. With such changes in the nature of migration itself, and in the larger geo-political context in which migration is taking place, there is an increased demand for exploring the migration experiences among communities. Key questions include how individuals make migration decisions, how attachments to home are kept, and how migrant children are raised. Such information can be collected with the use of qualitative methods that are best suited to assess the daily life practices of individuals. Further study of such variables should then be undertaken through quantitative means.

Second-generation immigrant children are the fastest growing segment of the U.S. population of children. Any research done among American children must take into account this important demographic finding. Immigrant children or American-born children of immigrants have experiences and needs that must be studied further in order for policy makers, social workers, and others involved in improving living standards of children to be adequately informed. Issues of identity, mobility, language, and assimilation are key factors that should be taken into account in the research conducted among this population subgroup.

For Palestinian children born in the U.S., identity formation can often present a challenge. The experience for some can be characterized as "caught between two worlds." In the U.S., they face conflict between their parents' values and those of American society, and at the same time, cannot internalize elements of an identity which has its roots in a diaspora that they did not experience. For Palestinian-American women, the negotiation of identity is an greater challenge because much of what is defined as "tradition" rests on their shoulders.

For Palestinian-American returnees, this conflict is not easily resolved as they continue to identify only partially with the local society and culture and where some are faced with the additional challenges of stigma and exclusion. Palestinian-American youth, perhaps even more so than their parents, are clear examples of the fact that identity does not arise spontaneously from lived geographic spaces.

What future trajectories the identity of Palestinian-Americans will take is a subject needing further research. With time, the local culture and society in more cosmopolitan West Bank cities like Ramallah may change and be modified by them, and through other means, to more readily absorb them. Or perhaps as a collectivity, they will continue to create a new emergent identity with an undefined space between here and there as its base.

Bibliography

Abunimeh, Ali. 2003. Personal communication, March.

Aswad, Barbara and Barbara Bilge, eds., 1996. *Family and Gender among American Muslims*. Philadelphia: Temple University Press.

Beenstock, Michael. 1993. *Failure to Absorb: Return-Migration by Immigrants into Israel*. Jerusalem: Maurice Falk Institute for Economic Research in Israel, Discussion Paper No. 93.04.

Cainkar, Louise. 1994. "Palestinian Women in American Society: The Interaction of Social Class, Culture and Politics." In Ernest McCarus ed., *The Development of Arab American Identity*. Ann Arbor: The University of Michigan Press, pp. 85–105.

———. 1998. *Meeting Community Needs, Building on Community Strengths: Chicago's Arab American Community*. Chicago, IL: Arab American Action Network.

Cainkar, Louise, Ali Abunimah, and Lamia Raei. 2004. "Migration as a Method of Coping with Turbulence among Palestinians," *Journal of Comparative Family Studies*, 35 (2):229–40.

Gmelch, George. 1992. *Double Passage: The Lives of Caribbean Migrants Abroad and Back Home.* Ann Arbor: University of Michigan Press.

King, Russell. 2000. "Generalizations from the History of Return Migration." In Bimal Ghosh, ed., *Return Migration: Journey of Hope or Despair?* Geneva: International Organization for Migration and the United Nations, pp. 7–55.

Licht, G. and V. Steiner. 1993. "Assimilation Labor Market Experience and Earnings Profiles of Temporary and Permanent Immigrant Workers in Germany," *International Review of Applied Economics* 8 (2):130–56.

Mandel, Ruth. 1990. "Shifting Centers and Emergent Identities: Turkey and Germany in the lives of Turkish *Gastarbeiter.*" In Eickelman, Dale and James Piscatori, eds., *Muslim Travelers: Pilgrimage, Migration and the Religious Imagination.* Berkeley: University of California Press, pp. 153–71.

Massey, Douglas, S. Rafael Alarcon, Jorge Durand, and Humberto Gonzalez. 1987. *Return to Aztlan: The Social Process of International Migration from Western Mexico.* Berkeley: University of California Press.

Portes, Alejandro and Ruben G. Rumbaut. 2001. *Legacies: The Story of the Immigrant Second Generation.* Berkeley: University of California Press.

Sayre, Ward and Jennifer Olmsted. 1999. "Economics of Palestinian Return Migration," *Middle East Report*, 212 (http://www.merip.org/mer/mer212/212_olmsted_sayre.html).

Suleiman, Michael W., ed. 1999. *Arabs in America: Building a New Future.* Philadelphia: Temple University Press.

Chapter 7
Virtual and Real Returns

Sari Hanafi

THE DISPERSION of a people due to forced emigration has traditionally been analyzed as a contributing factor in the creation of transnational networks. In this view, the initiation of a peace process should foster the re-establishment of local and international economic links after a long period of conflict. Using existing ties to the native community, diasporas are also seen as significant influences on the reshaping and emergence of new economic networks. In this respect, however, prevalent discourse about diasporic networks has tended toward overstatement, often to mythic proportions. Little attention has been paid to network absence or to networks ruptured due to structural constraints caused by various factors (such as the impermeability of inter-state borders, the absence of ties following prolonged separation, etc.).

The objective of this chapter is to evaluate the volume of the "return" to the Palestinian territories since the Oslo process began, and assess the contribution of expatriates to the development of the Palestinian territories since the Oslo agreements in terms of know-how and expertise. The focus will be on a UNDP program that encourages repatriation called TOKTEN (The Transfer of Knowledge Through Expatriate Nationals) combined with an analysis of an internet-based network, PALESTA (Palestinian Scientists and Technologists Aboard), which connects Palestinian scientists and professional expatriates to the Palestinian territories. The new media (like the internet) facilitate the connectivity of the diaspora with the place of origin and the concept of the homeland, so that virtual returns may be as significant as real ones.

The "Real" Return: A Mass of Different Socio-Economic Categories

Some lessons can be learned from the experience of "returnees" to the Palestinian territories during the Oslo period. This return took the form of a collective influx during two distinct periods, as opposed to an organized or planned individual return. The first was a forced movement provoked by the outbreak of the Gulf War and entailed the emigration of some 350,000 Palestinians from Kuwait and other Gulf countries (Hanafi 1997; ESCWA 1993). However, only 37,000 of those, who had preserved their rights as permanent residents in the West Bank and Gaza, were able to return (Isotalo 2002). The second period followed the launching of the peace process and involved a return migration from Arab countries, such as Egypt and Jordan, as well as Tunisia. Palestinians with a precarious legal status or those who benefited from a quota agreed upon between Israel and the Palestinian National Authority (PNA) comprised the majority in this latter period.[1] Cases of individual return from various countries were also observed.[2] These migrants, belonging to different socio-professional categories, were often qualified university graduates possessing technical skills acquired in the host countries (Zureik 1997).

Although there are no reliable estimates of the number of returnees residing in the Palestinian territories, there are some indicators. According to the 1997 census by the Palestinian Central Bureau of Statistics (PCBS), the

---

1 Those who returned with the PLO were mostly PLO members and their families. They returned in the beginning of 1994 to be involved in building the institutions of the PNA. There came to be tens of thousands of people on the state payroll (if one includes the security services). They were among the higher rank of the PNA administration. Roger Heacock described their weight as follows:

   In the ministries, the directors general are 460 in number according to the archivist of the presidential office, in fact, more like 1000. Up to 65 percent are returnees, depending on sources. The same goes for the perhaps 2000 directors in the ministries. They dominate the executive branch. On the other hand, the inside heavily dominates the Palestinian Legislative Council or parliament elected in 1996. Although the numbers vary depending on the number of years of exile which define a person as a returnee rather than a local, there are by all counts well over 50 locals in the 88-member body. But its head, speaker Ahmad Qrei', a returnee who was elected to the PLC from Jerusalem, in turn heavily dominates that body. (Heacock 2002).

2 Some were admitted in accordance with family reunification or temporary visitor visas. The latter have remained despite their irregular status vis-à-vis Israeli regulations.

total number of returnees was 267,355, constituting 10.5 percent of the total population (Malki and Shalabi 2000). Interviews with representatives of the PLO Department of Refugee Affairs indicate that at least 200,000 of those may have returned during the Oslo process. According to surveys by Shaml and the Birzeit University Households (Giacaman and Johnson 2002), returnees are more highly educated than non-returnees.[3] They also have more members in civil service employment and less in the private sector. Indeed, the government, UNRWA, and/or NGOs employ 57 percent of the returnees.

Any discourse concerning Palestinian return to the West Bank and Gaza Strip incorporates its share of paradox. "Returning" Palestinians who hail from areas that became Israel in 1948 have not realized a return to their native villages or cities; in their cases, "return" signifies a new migration. Furthermore, the "return movement" remains ephemeral as Israel still controls immigration to the territory and rarely grants residency to returnees: returnees, who generally possess a foreign passport, are considered tourists and are given three-month visas or often only one month visas when traveling across land borders. Even when they work in Palestinian areas, they can rarely acquire a work permit or residency and they must repeatedly exit and re-enter the country before the expiration of their visa in order to obtain a new one. Those who overstay their visa risk being permanently barred entry into Israel and, consequently, the territory.

These above distinctions are important not least because they will have an impact on the character of any eventual Palestinian state. As Roger Heacock has noted, if the return is to a "remembered" land (the West Bank and Gaza Strip) and not to the historical one (pre-1948 Palestine), then it is not a returnee state, but a settler state. The case of Bosnia-Herzegovina demonstrates that a state based on a merely livable experience (and this at the expense of history) is not necessarily a successful one. In contrast, Israel, with its half-century of existence based on a discontinuous memory and reconstructed history, has undoubtedly been a successful case of settler state-building (1999:57).

The return to the Palestinian territories pre-dates the Oslo process, and, if anything, was sparked by the Iraq-Kuwait War (1990–91). However, three

---

3   Generally, refugees in the Palestinian territories have higher levels of education than non-refugees. Fewer refugees are illiterate or with elementary skills (23 percent) compared to non-refugees (25 percent), have more secondary education (17 percent) compared to non-refugees (15 percent) and more post-secondary education (11 percent) compared to non-refugees (8 percent). This confirms the importance of UNRWA support for refugees, education and perhaps the refugee population's ambition to seek educational capital where other forms of capital do not exist. (Giacaman and Johnson 2002: 12).

quarters of those who responded to the Shaml survey indicated a post-Oslo return.[4] Half of those interviewed returned with the PNA, while 13 percent were beneficiaries of the family reunification policy. What is important here is that around a quarter of the returnees lack proper papers as they came as visitors and Israel has not permitted the renewal of stays in the Palestinian territories since the beginning of the second *intifada* in 2000. Return seems to have taken place in consultation with their families (81 percent); in only 10 percent of the cases did the family oppose a return, mainly because of spousal commitments abroad. In one case, the family accepted the decision of the father, but the women imposed the condition that they not take Palestinian IDs and keep their status as foreigners. It also appears that the opposition to return migration was not generally from spouses but mainly from the older children, who did not want to return.

According to the Shaml survey, returnees' situation improved after their return, although the nature of their jobs changed. While half previously worked as employees, 80 percent did so upon their return. Three quarters declared themselves satisfied with their work and only one quarter said their economic situation had worsened. These percentages should be read in the context of the general instability as a result of the *intifada*. Only a third received help from family members when they moved, largely because the majority were not originally from the West Bank or the Gaza Strip; therefore, they did not have family members there or a family which was able to help them financially.

Overall, three quarters declared that they were satisfied with their return, despite the difficulties. Older people were more satisfied than young people. The latter complained particularly about the level of health services, housing, and the quality of education.[5] Two-thirds still rent their apartments ten years after arrival.

Most importantly, even though two-thirds had expectations about the "homeland" *(al-watan)* which were different from what they encountered, this did not hinder 95 percent of them to advise others to come to the territory. Homeland becomes not just a "natural" place of return or a symbol of the *intifada* and political alienation, but a real place, where there are job opportunities and scientific and technological development. One female returnee

---

4   The Shaml survey is mentioned earlier in the introduction.

5   65 percent of the returnees interviewed spoke of encountering difficulties, mainly social ones, during their initial time. Around 41 percent said health services in the Palestinian territories were poor and only 22 percent said they were good. Many returnees complained about Palestinian universities as too commercial, but more than the half expressed satisfaction with their children's schools.

called it the "country of interest and of love… the last refuge for people after the tiring exile in countries that did not respect refugee rights." Many came to the homeland even if they were originally from historical Palestine. "It is not the homeland I had dreamed of and not my people to whom I thought I belonged," said one frustrated man, who returned on the PLO list after 1993.

Even if returnees were satisfied, the return experience was and will be problematic. Many have said that the local population did not welcome them or seemed not to want their return, especially in the West Bank. They saw the economic advantage of returning but found it difficult to adapt socially to the Palestinian society. An employee with the PNA administration stated, "We are different in culture and mode of thinking." Nonetheless, most respondents, especially in Gaza, viewed the return phenomenon as providing important advantages, including an increase in the number of educated people and intellectuals, the presence of multiple cultures in Palestine, and a revival of Islamic values. It is curious that in an overcrowded Gaza, return migration was seen as a way to increase the Palestinian population in the territory, an argument not made by Western bankers.

After dealing generally with all socio-economic categories of the Palestinian returnees, one should take into account that the movements of the professionals are more complicated and follow a different logic which imbricates both local and global levels. The magnitude of the (forced and voluntary) migration of scientists and, more widely, professionals has been increasing on a global level in the last three decades.[6] In the Palestinian case, such an outflow must be viewed in the context of the mass exodus of Palestinians since the creation of the Israeli state in 1948. It would be unwise to give an estimate of how great the volume of Palestinian professionals is since verifiable data is unfortunately unavailable. The research I conducted from 1996 to 1999 in many areas of the Palestinian diaspora, however, demonstrates important concentrations of professionals mainly in the Gulf, the U.S., Canada, and the UK. Recently, new clusters have emerged whose size has been increasing rapidly. Such a community can be found in Lille (France) where some 45 Palestinian professionals, mainly scientists and engineers, stayed on following their studies at Lille universities in the last decade. Such a phenomenon has its origin in professional diaspora networks, especially those involving science and technology professionals.

---

6   The SESTAT database of the United States National Science Foundation shows that in 1995, 1.4 million of the 12 million science and engineering professionals, who work in technology and engineering occupations in the USA, are of foreign origin. Over 72 percent of these foreign-born professionals originate from developing countries (Meyer and Brown, 1999:3).

Virtual Communities

The difficulty in finding a mechanism for the physical return of Palestinian refugees to their land of origin is increasingly being addressed by the rise of virtual communities. The crisis of social connectivity with the "homeland" which began with the installation of the Palestinian National Authority and a paradoxical and parallel physical inaccessibility to the "homeland," point to the urgency of a cyberspace connectivity project. For this reason, an internet-based network, PALESTA (Palestinian Scientists and Technologists Abroad), was established at the end of 1997 in order to "harness the scientific and technological knowledge of expatriate professionals for the benefit of development efforts in Palestine."[7]

Although PALESTA targets all Palestinian communities abroad, its main focus has been Europe and North America. It has thus neglected communities in the Arab world. The network functions as a discussion group as well as a database for information on skilled Palestinians living abroad.

While connectivity between the diaspora and the "homeland" is an important factor in fostering physical return, a temporary physical return also remains possible for skilled Palestinians, a category whose participation is vital to the construction of the Palestinian entity. In this case, is it possible for a voluntary facilitator role to be assumed by the Palestinian National Authority or the international community to harness this group and facilitate the transmission of expertise from the migrant community to the "homeland"? There are two possible policies for developing countries to tap their expatriate professional communities: either through a policy of repatriation (a return option), or through a policy of remote mobilization and connection to scientific, technological and cultural programs at home (a diaspora option). These two policies have both been employed in the Palestinian territories, the former through a UNDP program that encourages repatriation called TOKTEN (The Transfer of Knowledge Through Expatriate Nationals), and the latter through PALESTA. In this section we will focus only on the diaspora option. The study of the trajectory of PALESTA, as well as its strong and weak points, is very important to avoid the mistakes that have left PALESTA currently out of service in case it should be resumed in the future.[8]

---

7   For more information about this network, see (http://www.palesta.gov.ps/).

8   This study is based on much empirical and theatrical research including 54 interviews of Palestinian professionals in France and the UK conducted in 1998, focusing on their economic activities and their connectivity to the homeland. For an assessment of the impact of PALESTA in connecting the Palestinian diaspora (especially in Europe) with the Palestinian territories, I will use an evaluation of the PALESTA network in 2000, which

TOKTEN: A Tentative Step to Brain Gain?[9]

The TOKTEN concept is an interesting mechanism for tapping into national expatriate human resources and mobilizing them to undertake short-term consultancy work in their countries of origin. The UNDP, which founded it, created the program to utilize the expertise of expatriate nationals. Among other things, the program demonstrated that specialists abroad (who had migrated to other countries and achieved professional success there) were enthusiastic about providing short-term technical assistance to their country of origin, and might even be persuaded to return and resettle. The program has been implemented for over the last 22 years in 30 different countries, resulting in thousands of technical assistance missions by expatriate professionals to their home countries. Historically, the catalyst for TOKTEN was the "brain drain" from developing countries. The program created a database of highly trained and experienced expatriates and in the 1990s and 2000s assigned more than 500 of them, on a semi-volunteer basis,[10] to their countries of origin for anything from one month to six months. They have served governments, the public and private sector, universities, and NGOs.[11] Palestinian TOKTEN consultants, for example, have helped reform the treatment of kidney disease in the Palestinian territories and have guided the development of macro-economic frameworks and planning. TOKTEN skills have also made significant progress in the areas of computerization and information technology, on city planning, on university curriculum development and academic networking, on the upgrading of film and television capacities, and on cultural preservation, including the Bethlehem 2000 project.

The distribution of TOKTEN's experts from 1994 to 2001 by sector shows a major focus on strategic planning with around 43 percent. Other sectors include IT (14 percent), agriculture and water (12 percent), and health (10 percent) (www.tokten.org/images/cross.gif). The lack of expertise in some sectors where people have volunteered under TOKTEN has

---

was compiled through an analysis of the content of electronic mail messages exchanged between PALESTA's team and Palestinians abroad.

9 The author expresses his gratitude to Mounir Kleibo, program officer in UNDP, and Abeer Nusseibeh who provided information about TOKTEN for this study.

10 In the Palestinian territories, in addition to travel expenses and miscellaneous costs, a senior TOKTEN consultant receives $3,000 and a junior consultant receives $2,000.

11 In 1994, the Government of Norway contributed U.S.$350,000 to launch the TOKTEN Palestinian program and in 1996 the Government of France contributed U.S.$50,000 to place French speaking Palestinian expatriate professionals under the TOKTEN scheme. UNDP/PAPP also contributed U.S.$250,000 (core funds) for the TOKTEN program (bridging funds). Overall, the government of Japan has been the major contributor to the TOKTEN Palestinian program with a total of $4.2 million since 1996 (www.tokten.org).

generated some real success stories in Palestine, such as the construction and opening of the international airport in Gaza planned by TOKTEN consultants, nine of whom stayed on and formed the backbone of the airport's operations (UNDP 1999:1–2). Later, the major focus of TOKTEN placements became PNA reform.

Some 50 percent of the consultants came from Jordan (a country suffering from its own economic crisis but benefiting from an important science and technology community that graduated mainly from Western universities). Twenty percent came from the USA (where there is a large West Bank community that has close ties with the homeland) and Canada. Fifteen percent came from Europe (which constitutes a small percentage of the Palestinian community there, especially considering its relative geographical proximity to the Palestinian territories), and finally another 15 percent came from the Gulf region (this small percentage is due to the fact that knowledge of the program there is limited and the Palestinian community profits from good job opportunities already). These numbers are all from 2001. The picture now is quite different as the Israeli authority no longer allows professionals born in Arab countries to enter under the TOKTEN program. Thus the percentage of people from Jordan has become less significant.

The TOKTEN program in fact attracts more young experts than older ones. According to Mounir Kleibo (personal communication), around 80 percent of the experts are between 25 to 35 years old. Two conclusions can be drawn from that: first, the age-group is a more mobile one, and secondly, the money offered is not sufficient to attract people with more experience. Furthermore, younger people are more likely to be able to adapt to the tiring circumstances pertaining to the Palestinian territories. The ability to adapt is a very important quality as Israeli checkpoints and closures making the environment very hard for those less dynamic and mobile. Kleibo also argued that the failure of some program missions was mainly the responsibility of the Palestinian institutions on the ground and not the TOKTEN experts.

However, the success of the TOKTEN program should not only be measured by an increase in demand or the results of specific consultancies. The program provided these experts an opportunity to experience first-hand life in their native countries and encouraged them to settle there in the long-term.

In fact, the survey I conducted at the beginning of the 2000 *intifada* shows that about 21 percent of TOKTEN experts, or 34 out of 160, still live in the Palestinian territories after their TOKTEN assignment expired. The returnees came mainly from Jordan and the USA, two countries where the Palestinian community has maintained close links with their families in the West Bank and Gaza. It is a very high percentage for a country like Palestine where the political and economic situation is very difficult (see Table 1). Only Lebanon is comparable, where 16 percent (six out of 36) of TOKTEN experts settled after their mission was completed, and there these expatriates do not have any residency difficulties (Ghattas 1999). This percentage dropped to 12 percent in 2006 because of the *intifada* context (Kleibo 2007).

Table 1: Distribution of Returnees by Country of Origin

Country	Number of returnees
Jordan	15
USA	12
UK	2
Canada	1
UAE	1
France	2
Saudi Arabia	1
Total	**34**

The TOKTEN Palestinian program seems to have been very positive. It has been thoroughly reviewed by a mission from UNV headquarters conducted by Eva Ditmar, the conclusions of which supported the overall modality and its implementation in the West Bank and Gaza. The Sixth International TOKTEN Conference held in Beijing China over the period 7–11, May 2000, recognized the TOKTEN Palestinian program as the model for successful TOKTEN programs everywhere (See <www.tokten.org>). However, the program does have some weaknesses. Firstly, in the first 3 years, the beneficiaries of the TOKTEN program were mainly Palestinian ministries and public institutions, and the private sector and NGO's share of this expertise continues to be marginal. Since 1999, the TOKTEN management has been reconsidering its allocation to the NGO sector. Secondly, the selection of qualified candidates is problematic as there is not yet a large enough database capable of identifying expatriates willing to volunteer for technical assistance missions, except the one established by PALESTA that will be discussed later. In addition, the timing of the missions can be problematic, as TOKTEN experts need to be available when the recipient institution requires help. Direct dialogue through the internet of the three parties concerned is instrumental in ensuring expediency and success.

In some countries where international experts are employed, there are often suspicions that these experts are following the agendas of their own governments, but experts from the Palestinian diaspora do not appear to suffer from this problem. However, difficulties did arise when locals felt the "experts" had neither greater experience nor better qualifications yet were paid up to three times as much. This became even more problematic when some ministries, despite their limited budgets, asked the UNDP for TOKTEN experts when they discovered that they could not recruit permanent local employees with the right expertise.

Finally, the TOKTEN program raised the issue of whether the concept of "brain drain" could be tackled in the framework of the nation-state. With the process of globalization, the labor market has become increasingly internationalized and the question has arisen as to whether developing countries can compete with developed countries where wages are far higher. This situation seems to disadvantage these countries. For instance, the experience of India in terms of the globalization of Indian knowledge workers shows that it has not been very gainful to that country. According to Khadria (1999:150–56), in spite of the fact that remittances have been quite significant, especially in relation to the balance of payments problem, "...the payments made by developing countries to developed countries on technology account would be in the vicinity of U.S. \$10 billion per annum, canceling at one stroke a major part of the total aid flow from the latter to the former," as the remittances are considered as returns on capital invested for training.

TOKTEN could provide a mechanism whereby the recipient countries of migration (usually the western countries) can compensate the country of emigration. Some western governments have given grants to their migrant communities so that they can explore the possibility of returning to their homeland. For example, the German government subsidized two missions of a Palestinian-German medical delegation. One of these missions allowed two Palestinian doctors to settle back in Palestine after it was over. However, these mechanisms are not sufficient and the international community has to find a more radical solution, for example by regulating the global skills market in order to control the disastrous effects of this globalization of labor on the developing countries. In its report of 1999, the World Bank (2000) advised regulation of the global skills market, but no proper measures have yet been taken.

PALESTA Network: A Virtual Return

This section undertakes a study of the relationship between networking and new media (especially the internet) in the context of a unique internet-based network of connectivity among Palestinian professionals and the Palestinian entity called PALESTA (Palestinian Scientists and Technologists Abroad).

The PALESTA network utilizes cyberspace, embodied by the communications technology of the internet, as its conduit. In this case, the internet can be viewed not just as a tool, but as a distinct and new environment of connectivity between various Palestinian communities in the diaspora and the homeland. As Holmes argues, it is the "context which brings about new corporealities and new politics corresponding to new space-worlds and new time-worlds" rather than solely "instruments in the service of pre-given bodies and communities" (1997: 4).

PALESTA has undergone two major stages: in the first stage, it constituted a center, functioning as a server based in Palestine and connecting to individuals in different peripheries. In the second stage, it aided in the creation of different nodes in countries where there is a concentration of Palestinian professionals while still remaining at the center of connectivity. The latest discussions within PALESTA indicate that there is a desire to make it less central, transforming it into a node within a series of nodes. (For these stages see Figures 1 and 2.) However, since 2001, PALESTA has been hibernating for different reasons, mainly due to lack of funding.

PALESTA Network's First Phase: A Centralized Model

While the return of skilled and professional individuals has been marginal under TOKTEN's low capacity programs, the ambitious PALESTA network project sought to more directly connect a larger group of professionals in the diaspora to the center. It has the objective of harnessing the scientific and technological knowledge of Palestinian expatriate professionals for the benefit of development efforts in Palestine. There are two other similar pioneering networks that deal with South Africa and Colombia: SANSA (South African Network of Skills Abroad), and Red Caldas (the Network of Colombian Technologists and Scientists Abroad) (Meyer et al. 1999).

PALESTA's network, a hybrid constructed by the Palestinian Ministry of Planning and International Cooperation's (MOPIC) Science and Technology Planning Unit with UNDP support, was launched in 1997. The network includes a database of expatriate Palestinian scientists and professionals and a discussion forum for participants to contribute their technical knowledge and experience in addressing important issues in the development of the Palestinian economy. The network functions as a kind of professional gateway providing current job listings and developments in many public, private, and NGO institutions in the Palestinian territories, as well as workshops and public events. It has set itself three objectives. The first is to involve expatriate Palestinian scientists and technologists in serious discussions aimed at resolving scientific and technological problems vital to Palestinian economic development. The second is to keep expatriate Palestinians informed about developments and programs at home in the areas of science and technology so that they will be prepared to contribute fully when their presence is needed in Palestine. The final objective is to obtain the assistance of these expatriates in identifying and initiating new projects that will contribute to aspects of Palestinian economic development.

PALESTA sought to become a familiar powerful tool among decision makers in Palestine and expatriate science and technology professional communities. By ensuring a high level of quality in operation, establishing familiarity among relevant communities, and providing a structure amenable to decentralization, it sought to continue its development into a viable and sustainable entity capable of making significant contributions to Palestinian development. Despite PALESTA's ambitious objectives, however, current analysis of the network demonstrates mixed results.[12] Following its launch in 1997, PALESTA had two stages: first as a centralized institution (1997–1999) and then as decentralized network allowing connectivity between periphery/periphery (1999–2001), before entering hibernation.

Profile of PALESTA members: Representative of the diaspora? Two years after being launched, PALESTA's database of expatriate Palestinian professionals contained 1,300 expatriate Palestinian professionals. However, only a third (some 480 professionals) are active members of PALESTA with updated contact information. According to a PALESTA survey,[13] its active membership is concentrated in the United States (56 percent of total

---

12 This section uses findings from a previous evaluation conducted by the author. The methodology of the evaluation was comprised of the following steps: 1) Interviews conducted in January 2000 of PALESTA staff as well as those involved in the elaboration of the PALESTA project, including the previous manager of PALESTA. Some PALESTA moderators were interviewed and were asked about their feelings and opinions concerning the functioning of the PALESTA network; 2) a review of the correspondence between PALESTA members in order to assess the impact of the discussion forum, 3) a review of progress reports submitted by PALESTA staff to the UNDP, as well as minutes of PALESTA staff meetings; and 4) interviews conducted with PALESTA members abroad and local PALESTA beneficiaries about their feelings and opinions concerning the network's services.

13 PALESTA distributed a questionnaire to members concerning their opinion on the PALESTA network in October 1999. Sixty PALESTA subscribers participated in the survey, (a response rate of 18.4 percent). The survey provided PALESTA with its first opportunity to identify member profiles in terms of academic qualifications, ages, country of residence, and so on.

PALESTA members), while only 17 percent live in Europe. PALESTA has not apparently been able to make inroads into Europe despite the continent's geographical proximity to Palestine. Its popularity in United State compared to Europe is probably due to the fact that Palestinian-American migrants mostly originate from the Palestinian territories, where PALESTA is based, while the Palestinians in Europe generally originate from historical Palestine. The Gulf and Jordan are similarly underrepresented (each representing only two percent of PALESTA membership). The survey also shows that PALESTA membership is relatively young: more than 37 percent are between the ages of 30–39, and 30 percent are between 20–29. They are highly educated: 41 percent of PALESTA members hold a doctorate degree, while 15 percent have a master degree. Women are overwhelmingly underrepresented, constituting only 7 percent of PALESTA members.

"Who owns PALESTA?" The architecture of the first phase of the PALESTA system has had significant effects on both the subject matters covered within the network and, more importantly, the construction of the identity of users in relation to the Palestinian homeland.

In light of the serious difficulty of free movement for Palestinians from the diaspora to the Palestinian territories, the PALESTA discussion forum constitutes a very important means of opening dialogue between geographically distant individuals in a cost-effective manner. Despite PALESTA's objective of discussing technical issues related to Palestinian economic development, however, the analysis of the content of messages posted by professionals residing abroad is more concerned with political and practical issues. The PALESTA forum has been instrumental in raising important discussions regarding social, political, and cultural issues such as eventual return or visits by expatriates to the Palestinian territories. A discussion concerning the contribution of the diaspora to Palestinian development (in which 121 messages were posted by members), highlights the perception of problems concerning the PNA's mismanagement of the Palestinian economy and its inability to convince Palestinian entrepreneurs in the diaspora to invest in the Palestinian territories. Furthermore, the content revealed that while the realization of PALESTA's objectives seems reliant on a form of unconditional assistance and participation from the diaspora for the new Palestinian quasi-state, diaspora members for their part were ready to lend this assistance only after matters of "practicality" were discussed.

Some messages were concerned with the issue of the second and third generations of the diaspora in western countries where youth have not always had access to Arabic language education (in this regard, summer camps for young people were suggested). Conversely, for Palestinians residing in the Palestinian territories, issues, such as second-generation diaspora, transnational Palestinian migration, and even assimilation of some groups abroad in the host countries, were conspicuously absent. Thus, while many issues regarding culture, politics, economy, education, and health were discussed in far greater depth than the intended topics of strict technical expertise and economic participation, PALESTA seemed incapable of taking into consideration its members' expectations by altering its objectives and the mode of their implementation.

One discussion in particular reveals the depth of PALESTA's crisis in the conception of its discussion list. In a discussion entitled "Who owns the list?" participating members expressed irritation over the so-called "editing" carried out by PALESTA staff. Many respondents considered the intervention to be a form of censorship rather than "editing." Moreover, participants voiced their desire to know each other, an option which PALESTA, both in conception and implementation, does not allow: each message is first sent to the network server, and subsequently posted without contact information by the network moderator. The intense nature of the discussion finally convinced PALESTA staff to circulate a questionnaire in October 1999 asking members their opinion about the network.

In terms of the stated goal and importance of launching discussions between local and expatriate Palestinians, the discussion also revealed some problems in PALESTA's mode of function and its structure. About 15 percent of PALESTA's subscribers have withdrawn from the discussion list.

The problem with the PALESTA model. The most fundamental criticism one can direct at PALESTA was that it functioned as an institution and not as a network. An institution is a hierarchical model of connectivity while the concept of network requires a horizontal one. PALESTA sought to connect members to the network without connecting members to each other. This formulation neglected the importance of developing and linking Palestinian communities in each country to one another. The objectives of such a network have been to prevent the total assimilation into host societies and ensure the preservation of a Palestinian heritage; such linkage, in turn, could facilitate contact with the Palestinian territories. Obviously such connectivity is impossible if its members are not allowed to know one another's email addresses. The contradiction highlights a paradoxical relationship between PALESTA's trans-geographical network and the content of the initial discourse produced by PALESTA managers concerning a geographically and biologically defined identity: a Palestinian abroad need only be connected to the center.

Additional issues were raised: how should PALESTA respond to non-Palestinian Arabs desiring to aid in the construction of a Palestinian state? How should it distinguish between a Jordanian and a Palestinian living in Jordan since both carry the same nationality? Furthermore, from a practical point of view, by centralizing its discussion list, PALESTA may have hindered its most effective method of reaching out to the Palestinian community abroad. The survey demonstrated that about half of the members discovered PALESTA through their relatives and friends, and 85 percent subsequently attempted to spread this information further. Thus, face-to-face relationships even in the era of cyberspace are significant. The virtual community does not spontaneously generate; factors of traditional physical and Cartesian space remain very important.

PALESTA's Second Phase: PALESTA as a Central Node

Though PALESTA members number more than a 1,000, the data suggests that only 20 percent participate regularly in email exchanges. Numerous discussions were launched in PALESTA's weekly staff meetings during the first six months of setup about the centralization of the discussion list. A number of team members expressed fear that unmitigated discussion groups might violate ethical standards of discourse and codes of conduct and could easily degenerate into school room debates filled with inappropriate language. Such a situation would cause frustration among serious users, and eventually discourage use of the discussion list. This argument for centralization was not conceived necessarily as authoritarian; rather it held that an unmonitored discussion list was not appropriate in terms of PALESTA's objectives. After its first year in operation (1998), however, it became clear to PALESTA's board that a moderating role raised more problems than it resolved. The board decided instead to impose sanctions against members who violated PALESTA's stated code of ethics. The PALESTA board took into account a common fear of the centralization of power among Palestinians abroad as well as those inside Palestine. The negative experiences of the diasporic Palestinians at the mercy of the political power of Arab regimes made them especially wary of censorship and monitoring. Though more reflective of a generalized phobia rather than a real concern, this fear expressed by many Palestinians abroad to the board compelled PALESTA to forgo their concerns and open the discussion list to allow contact between various members without facilitation by the PALESTA server. This change in the mode of operation after two years of operation (1999) was fundamental. PALESTA's new mode of connectivity has finally given Palestinians abroad a window for reconnecting people inside each community, and enabled users to bring about more substantial discussions (technical and general one) about the contribution of the Palestinian diaspora to the development of the Palestinian territories. PALESTA also became an important medium for recruiting Palestinian experts for different projects of development. The TOKTEN program, for instance, has extensively used the PALESTA database to identify competent people, instead of a selection based on clientelism or nepotism. Many discussions were even useful for the orientation of development projects without participants having to come to the Palestinian territories. While this has generated great interest in PALESTA, the members I interviewed expressed again a lack of information about how to become involved. Many also expressed a desire to see PALESTA become even less centralized (less of an institution and more of a network).

In its second phase, PALESTA was successful in encouraging the creation of various global network nodes in order to facilitate contact with and between expatriate Palestinians. Though professionals sometimes appear isolated from their Palestinian communities in almost all western countries, the creation of nodes for professional Palestinians has been an important factor for the recruitment of PALESTA members. During 1999, there were numerous Palestinian community conferences and activities in the United States and Europe among periphery-periphery groups that reinforced the dynamics of this perspective. The first meeting of the Palestinian Canadian Professional Association in 1999 was one example, whereby the benefit of the openness of the PALESTA mailing list was evident. In Europe, a meeting of the Palestinian engineers and professionals was held in the offices of UNESCO (Paris) in March 1999 under the auspices of PALESTA.

PALESTA's previous experience, however, reveals a low capacity to recruit new members individually. In fact, many factors related to the persistence of a centralized management of PALESTA have generated certain inertia. Thus, in spite of the relative openness of its mailing list, PALESTA continued to privilege a mode of connectivity of center (the homeland) to periphery (countries of the diaspora) and hinder the full blossoming of periphery-periphery relationships. This issue, among other internal ones, led to PALESTA suspending operations in 2001, less than two years after the beginning of the second phase, due to organizational and funding reasons. This does not mean that the project has failed since we must take into account the consequences of the *intifada* that have been so detrimental to the functioning of all PNA ministries and administrations.

Output and limits of PALESTA

The experience of PALESTA demonstrates the increasing importance of Palestinian professional diaspora networks. PALESTA's electronic discussion list has had a positive and direct effect on providing space and form to help the PNA in its state construction phase. Typically, this was planned to happen through the moderator who would propose to the mailing list in general (or specific PALESTA member belonging to certain sectors) to address various problems directly. After a month of discussion, a suitable expert—who was either hired or served on a voluntary basis—was identified and s/he came to the Palestinian territories to resolve the particular problem. This happened many times and beneficiaries were sometimes from the private and industrial sectors. Advertised job vacancies in the Palestinian territories also allowed many of PALESTA's members to apply when abroad. Some of them now have contracts thanks to these ads. Indeed, many Palestinian universities have hired teachers through PALESTA.

The network has also, in a limited way, created a tangible social space that has generated a kind of collective self-conscious for a worldwide professional expatriate community. Communication through PALESTA, or any other similar network, allows mutual identification for actors and allows inferences to be made concerning their associations. However, the virtual community has its limits. A critical examination reveals a tendency, as Willson suggests (1997: 158), of "thinning the complexities of human engagement to the level of a one-dimensional transaction and a detaching of the user from the political and social responsibilities of the real space environment." The subject in cyberspace tends to become, to paraphrase Baudrillard, "a mere screen for the assimilation of data" (Cooper 1997:100). The technology of new media, like the internet, is not a panacea for the lack of physical connectivity of the Palestinian diaspora. PALESTA's weak overall effect reflects an over-reliance on a technological approach where connectivity is based mainly on electronic exchange through which very few forms of actual physical contact or concrete projects are launched via the network. As Heidegger noted, function does not necessarily produce activity. "Everything is functioning. This exactly is what is so uncanny, that everything is functioning and that the functioning drives us more and more to even further functioning" (Cooper 1997:98). While the PALESTA network is functioning on the level of electronic connectivity, daily email exchanges will not necessarily generate activity on the individual or collective part of its members. It appears that a minimum physical and face-to-face contact is indispensable for generating activities.

Furthermore, communication should not be reduced to technical progress and "progress" cannot surpass cultural and social changes. There is certainly a danger that electronic connectivity gives supremacy to technology, which may instrumentalize communication. In such a context, it would be difficult to distinguish between inherent value and the interests of actors. The effect of new communication technology cannot be analyzed without being situated in the framework of the society, and all theories of communication must take into account the existing bonds of a society. Communication theory necessitates societal theory.

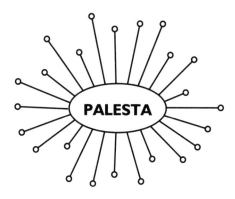

Figure 1: PALESTA's First Stage: Connectivity to the individuals

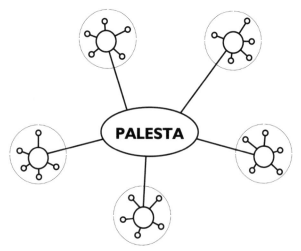

Figure 2: PALESTA's Second Stage: Central with different nodes

New Media and Reshaping the Palestinian Identity
After presenting the limits and the potentials of PALESTA, it is very important to question its impact on the perception and the position of the homeland for the diasporic communities.

New media, homeland, and subjectivity. As Giddens points out, one of the consequences of the evolution of modernity is the resulting separation of time and space from place, which creates what he calls "disembedded" social systems or the "lifting out" of social relations from local contexts of interaction and their "restructuring across indefinite spans of time-space" (1990:21). In this era of globalization, the relationship of the individual to the homeland becomes relative. Nevertheless, the idea of "the homeland" remains in some form within the minds of exiled Palestinians—a notion regularly updated by the content of a steady flow of satellite television channels (al-Jazeera, al-Arabiyya, and MBC) beaming daily images from the occupied land. Connectivity with the Palestinian homeland now involves a complex process composed of varying levels of virtual and physical social networks. The difficulty of achieving physical connectivity has given birth to a virtual reality, which now constitutes a new form of social relationship. Contrary to those who think that the internet will impose a cosmopolitan identity, cyberspace instead promotes new possibilities of re-anchoring culture and identity in the local, thereby reinforcing ethnic identity and always in ways that bypass the constraints of society.

PALESTA specifies a discourse oriented towards a group defined not only by a national identity, but by a professional one as well. The homeland is expected to offer both national and professional inspiration. Through mechanisms of connectivity, such as TOKTEN and PALESTA, what becomes important is not only the right of return, but also the utility of the homeland for the diaspora. While the homeland is no longer an abstract idea, Palestinian resources have not yet been developed to a level that would allow a generous plan of insertion, such as has been the case for Jewish diaspora and immigrants vis-à-vis Israel.

Interviewing PALESTA members who are expatriates or returnees, I was struck by the emergence of the subject of return in their discourse. The Palestinian homeland, as a symbolic icon of service and sacrifice, no longer supersedes the self but is instead often perceived as a homeland that can be served while the individual pursues a social position within it. It has become clear that service to the homeland need not be separated from the personal desire for a better life. The posture is a clear expression of subjectivity quite different from the predominant discourse of mass media, which depicts the

Palestinians in the diaspora as refugees intending only to sacrifice for the benefit of the homeland. In this regard, interviewees often express feelings of dissonance before achieving connectivity via new electronic media. Before, they had felt a level of guilt for not actively engaging in some activity for the benefit of the homeland, while concurrently experiencing feelings of commitment to their life in a host country that did not necessarily allow them freedom of movement to the homeland. While the physical mobility of the diasporic Palestinians is completely hindered, the circulation of ideas, feelings, and expertise through PALESTA has become very important. This circulation touches everything: development in Palestine, the kind of infrastructure that the Palestinian society should have for receiving the children born in the diaspora, issues of democracy and multiculturalism, etc. In spite of the physicality of geography, the virtual connectivity has impacted on the identity construction of both the population in the Palestinian territories and in the diaspora. The PALESTA network seemed capable of creating a fluid dynamic of construction, deconstruction, representations, and symbols. The homeland is no longer synonymous only with *intifada* and political alienation, but also with job opportunities, scientific and technological development, specialist conferences, and so on. Palestinian identity has moved beyond a completely territorialized framework. One can be a Palestinian abroad, connecting with and aiding the development of the homeland in cyberspace.

The new media technologies discussed here seem to encourage individualization. Palestinian actors are no longer necessarily united in the social and political spheres, not because of the elimination of the ideological world, but because human agency has radically changed its spatial, temporal, and technological existence. The environment of cyberspace implies highly individualized forms of social bonds with an attendant atomization of populations within the confines of the workstation or the borders of the homepage. In such a context, connectivity through new media cannot be solely conceived of as bringing individuals and groups into contact; it also addresses their differences by amplifying representations of the individual. Networking can enhance subjectivity in an environment where various voices are expressed independently regardless of the relative importance of their respective social positions. It is interesting to note the fault line of divergence between PALESTA members concerning a discussion of the role of the Palestinian government in development. It is not shaped by the habitual discussion where the actors position themselves as loyal to the Palestinian National Authority (favoring the dominant faction, Fatah) or as an ally of the opposition (the other political factions), but where they shape their position through their experience as individuals acquired in the host country.

A diaspora with a weak center of gravity. If PALESTA's strength in recruiting members has been its capacity to function in different nodes at the periphery-periphery level (but always with a tendency to keep a center), it seems that it was able to connect different parts of the Palestinian diaspora even though the structure of this diaspora is very problematic because of its weak center of gravity (Hanafi 2003). What are the meanings and implications of a diaspora with a weak center of gravity? I will argue that the weak center of gravity in the Palestinian case would eventually play a deciding role in the decline of Palestinian-ness in the long term, but new media will partially compensate for this problem.

A classic diaspora is defined by a center of gravity which has two functions: it channels the flow of communications between diaspora members in different peripheries, while it also provides a location where members (especially family) can meet. The first function does not necessarily require a physical site; the meeting location might be a service provider or institution such as the National Jewish Fund for world Jewry, the Tunisian base of the PLO for Palestinians, and the PKK in Germany in the Kurdish case. In regard to the second function, a physical geographical location is a necessity and an important factor for community economic transactions. Thus, the center of gravity has nothing to do with the symbolic weight of a mythical or real homeland. It is a center for connecting members of the diaspora who belong to the same economic and social networks. In this respect, historical Palestine continues to fill an important role in the imagination of the Palestinian diaspora, although not necessarily playing a role for everybody living abroad.

My research on Palestinian entrepreneurs in the diaspora demonstrates the importance of a physical meeting place. A Palestinian originally from Nazareth (as Nazareth kept its Arab population), for example, can have a very active economic network based in Nazareth capable of drawing those from Canada, the U.S., or Australia for meetings with the remaining Palestinians in the town. In contrast, Palestinians originating from Haifa (an example of a city in which virtually all the Arab population was deported by Israeli forces in 1948) do not have access to such a network due to the absence of any relatives there. Such inaccessibility to the territorial reference point effectively hinders the possibility of meeting. A Haifa family dispersed throughout Damascus, Montreal, Amman, and Abu Dhabi would have little interest in meeting in Syria where only one member of the family lives. Those in Arab countries may also find the cost of traveling to Canada or the Gulf prohibitive, long before the equally daunting dilemma of acquiring a visa ever enters into the discussion. These torn networks, due to the absence of territorial reference, are not exclusive to the Palestinians. They have also been noted in the case of Gypsies who migrated from Paris to New York. Williams (1987) reports that only a few years after this migration, the family relationships of those Gypsies broke down.

The total inaccessibility of historical Palestine makes it impossible for it to function as a center of gravity. Since this is the case, might the Post-Oslo Palestinian territories play this role? This territory would be considered as the "natural" center of gravity for Palestinians. A combination of factors, however, has prevented it from assuming this role. It is not accessible to the majority of Palestinians abroad, while in addition many members in the Palestinian diaspora have lost confidence in the Palestinian National Authority's efficacy for state-building. Though the diaspora has played a major role in the national issue and in supporting the PLO during 50 years of resistance, it has consciously refused to transform its role into that of "a Rothschild." Though willing to support the homeland economically and financially, the diaspora also seeks a decision-making role regarding the process of institution-building.

In this context of a weak center of gravity, the new media like PALESTA can partially compensate by allowing communication between different communities of a diaspora without this communication necessarily going through the center. However, as already argued, such functioning was burdened by the team of PALESTA who wanted to keep the role of the center as the most important.

Conclusion

There are paradoxes and serious problems when the relationship between the diaspora and the place of origin is reduced to cyberspace networking without genuine efforts of promoting activities. Encouraged by the new information technologies, Manuel Castells described the network society as a shift from social groups to social networks. But these networks are neither obvious nor neutral (Latour 1999). In his seminal book Liquid Love, Zygmunt Bauman (2003) noticed that people speak ever more often of connections, of connecting and being connected, rather than reporting their experiences and prospects in terms of relating and relationships. Instead of talking about partners, they prefer to speak of networks. Unlike relationships and partnerships, which stand for mutual engagement over disengagement, network stands for a matrix for simultaneously connecting and disconnecting. In a network, connecting and disconnecting are equally legitimate choices and carry the same importance. Network suggests moments of "being in touch" interspersed with periods of free roaming. In a network, connections are entered on demand, and can be broken at will. Does that constitute a summary of the history of PALESTA?

The PALESTA network and the diaspora option (the policy of remote mobilization and connection to scientific, technological and cultural programs at home), seem to be a real and workable proposition for turning the negative effects of forced emigration into tangible benefits. Such an approach also concretely addresses the problems that brain drain countermeasures have been unable to address (Meyer et al. 1999). PALESTA has undergone two major stages. In the first, it constituted a center, functioning as a server based in Palestine and connecting to individuals in different peripheries. In the second, it aided in the creation of different nodes in countries where there is a concentration of Palestinian professionals, while still remaining at the center of connectivity. Discussions within PALESTA indicated that there was a desire to make it less centralized and transform it into a node within in a series of nodes. These discussions are in abeyance as the network is suspended.

Contrary to the old Asian proverb that "falling leaves always return to their roots," Palestinian professionals do not engage in a massive return movement, while the "return" is still heavily controlled by the Israeli occupation. Instead of a physical return, I have endeavored to demonstrate that another form of "return," the virtual one, based on the PALESTA experience, has emerged. In this context, there is a sense of both the possibilities and the limitations of the PALESTA network and the new media technologies. PALESTA, as I have argued, had significant implications for "charting diasporic movements across national borders," as Shohat argued concerning an Iraqi diaspora discussion list (1999:231). Networking through the internet, as experienced through PALESTA, does not suggest the "end of geography," but a kind of "reshaping of geography" by connecting the different dispersed communities not only to the center but also between each other. If the process of construction and reconstruction of Palestinian identity can be largely effected by dispersed people with a fragile center of gravity (the Palestinian territories) to which almost all of the dispersed refugee communities cannot have access, the new media can be a very important tool for connecting these communities to each other without having to go through the center.

Yet this new medium functions both exclusively and inclusively. There is a risk of exclusiveness, as the target group for the new media is highly educated and most likely middle-class (rather than a general cross-section of the entire population). In addition, the target group is narrowed even more significantly because only those highly educated persons who are capable of reading and writing English may make use of it. This may explain why PALESTA not only has few members in Arab countries, but also in France and Germany. Such networks, however, also have a great potential for inclusion because the connection need not be necessarily based on an official connection between the PNA (or PLO popular organizations) and the Palestinian communities abroad. One can imagine the creation of multiple networks like PALESTA, representing various unaligned constituencies. Furthermore, cyberspace allows not only the globalization of cultural space but also its personalization. PALESTA, like other virtual networks, can facilitate democratic forms of interaction ("cyberdemocracy") as "it puts cultural acts, symbolizations in all forms, in the hands of all participants and thus radically decentralizes the positions of speech, publishing, filmmaking, radio and television broadcasting, in short the apparatuses of cultural production" (Poster 1997:234).

The impact of PALESTA on the relation between Palestinians abroad and the Palestinian territories goes beyond the simple effect of serving the homeland and facilitating a future physical return. In a transnational world typified by a process of global circulation of images, sounds, and goods, but not by a parallel free mobility of people, there has been a complex impact on the concept of communal belonging. We must ask, as Shohat has (1999:215), what do we make out of the new media's promise of shaping new identities? Furthermore, from a more radical perspective, will this new form of international migration alter our perception of the homogeneity of the nation and particularly the relationship between state, nation, and territory (Ma Mung et al. 1998:3)? In fact PALESTA's experience demonstrates that it contributes to the de-sanctification of the homeland by its de-terrorialization. Its members do not look for a "holy land" of ancestors, but for a land where they find a place that fits their profession and their expertise.

Homeland is a utopia in Mannheim's definition: once we have entered it, it disappears. The Palestinian return to Palestine has not necessarily taken place in a geographic location. Instead, the return has sought to incorporate itself within nodes of a network where the connectivity to a land of origin can be maintained.[16] The new media are likewise capable of facilitating conciliation between the diverse cultural heritages represented in the Palestinian diaspora by living in the host country while connecting to an inaccessible (and perhaps idealized) homeland. New media may broaden the ontological question: "Who am I?" with a kind of topographical identity question: "Where am I?"

---

16 In fact, here I do not address the legal or political dimensions of the location of a Palestinian state, which includes the West Bank, Gaza, and East Jerusalem, or the return of Palestinian refugees to their homeland with compensation. I am concerned with the sociological issue related to the right of choice for Palestinians to live in the place of origin or in the host country.

Bibliography

Bauman, Zygmunt. 2003. *Liquid Love: On the Frailty of Human Bonds.* Cambridge: Polity Press.

Cooper, S. 1997. "Plenitude and alienation: the subject of virtual reality." In D. Holmes, ed., *Virtual Politics. Identity and Community in Cyberspace.* London: Sage, pp. 87–109.

Ghattas, Kim .1999. "Expatriates on the move home, sweet home," (Report), www. tokten.com/employ.htm.

Giacaman, Rita and Penny Johnson, eds. 2002. *Inside Palestinian Household: Initial Analysis of a Community-based Household Survey.* Birzeit: Birzeit University, Volume One.

Giddens, Anthony. 1990. *The Consequences of Modernity.* Cambridge: Polity Press.

Hanafi, Sari. 1997. *Entre Deux Mondes. Les hommes d'affaires palestiniens de la diaspora et la construction de l'entité palestinienne.* Cairo: CEDEJ.

———. 2003. "Rethinking the Palestinians abroad as a diaspora: the relationships between the diaspora and the Palestinian territories," *HAGAR International Social Science Review,* 4 (1–2):78–110.

Heacock, Roger. 1999. *The Becoming of Returnee States: Palestine, Armenia, Bosnia.* Birzeit: Beirzeit Univeristy.

———. 2002. *Al-mahalliun wal 'aidun:* Locals and Returnees in the Palestinian National Authority (PNA), in http://www.birzeit.edu/research/locals.html.

Holmes, D. 1997. "Introduction: Virtual Politics, Identity and Community in Cyberspace." In D. Holmes, ed., *Virtual Politics: Identity and Community in Cyberspace.* London: Sage, pp. 4–23.

Latour, Bruno. 1999. "On Recalling ANT." In John Law and John Hassard, eds., *Actor Network Theory and After.* Oxford: Blackwell.

Kleibo, Mounir. 2007. "Professional Expatriate Palestinians Building their Homeland," unpublished paper.

Khadria, Binod. 1999. *The Migration of Knowledge Workers: Second-Generation Effects of India's Brain Drain.* New Delhi: Sage Publications.

Ma Mung, E., M.K. Doraï, F. Loyer, and M. Hily. 1998. "La circulation migratoire. Bilan des travaux," *Migrations Etudes,* 84: 3–16.

Malki, Majdi and Yasser Shalabi. 2000. *Internal Migration and Palestinian Returnees in West Bank and Gaza Strip.* Ramallah: MAS.

Meyer, J.B., J. Charum, D. Bernal, J. Gaillard, J. Granés, J. Leon, A. Montenegro, A. Morales, C. Murcia, and N. Narvaez-Berthelemot. 1999. *Turning Brain Drain Into Brain Gain: The Colombian Experience of the Diaspora Option.* Online at www. uct.ac.za/sansa/

Poster, M. 1997. "Cyberdemocracy: The Internet and the Public Sphere." In D. Holmes, ed., *Virtual Politics: Identity and Community in Cyberspace.* London: Sage, pp. 201–34.

Shohat, E. (1999) "By the Bitstream of Babylon, cyberfrontiers and Diasporic Vistas." In N. Hamid, ed., *Home, Exile, Homeland: Film, Media and the Politics of Place*. London: Routledge, pp. 212–32.

Williams, P. 1987. "Les couleurs de l'invisible: Tsiganes dans la banlieue parisienne? " In J. Gutwirth and C. Petonnet, eds., *Chemins de la Ville. Enquêtes Ethnologiques*. Paris: CTHS, pp. 53–73.

Willson, M. 1997. "Community in the abstract: a political and ethnical dilemma?" In D. Holmes, ed., *Virtual Politics: Identity and Community in Cyberspace*. London: Sage, pp. 121–39.

United Nations-ESCWA. 1993. *Return Migration. Profiles, Impact and Absorption*. New York: United Nations.

UNDP. 2000. "A Four-Year Brain Gain," draft UNDP Document. Jerusalem: UNDP.

Zureik, Elia. 1997. "The Trek Back Home: Palestinians Returning Home and their Problem of Adaptation." In Are Hovdanak, et al., eds., *Constructing Order: Palestinian Adaptation to Refugee Life*. Oslo: Institute for Applied Social Science (FAFO).

World Bank. 2000. *World Development Report: 1999/2000*. Washington: World Bank.

Note on the Contributors

Dr. Sari Hanafi is Associate Professor in the Department of Social and Behavioral Science, American University of Beirut, and chief editor of "Idafat: The Arab Journal of Sociology." From 2000 to 2005 he was director of the Palestinian refugee and Diaspora Center, Shaml, and in 1998 he was a cofounder of PALESTA.

Ms. Sheerin al-Araj has an MA in the Theory and Practice of Human Rights from the University of Essex, UK, 2006. Among other posts, she was associate researcher at the Palestinian Refugee and Diaspora Center, Shaml, in 2002-03. She is active in various social issues around her home base of Jerusalem.

Dr. Mary Totry has an MA in Sociology and a Phd in Political Science, both from the University of Haifa, where she teaches. She is the head of Civic Studies at Oranim College.

Dr. Cédric Parizot is an anthropologist and is based at the Centre de Recherche Français de Jérusalem and affiliated to the Institut de Recherche et d'Etudes sur le Monde Arabe et Musulman (IREMAM) in Aix-en-Provence.

Dr. Mohamed Kamel Doraï is a geographer and researcher at the French National Research Center (CNRS). He is currently working on migration issues at the Institut Français du Proche-Orient in Damascus.

Ms. Tamara Tamimi has an MA in Social Anthropology from Binghamton University. She is currently working for an international development firm in Amman, Jordan and travels frequently to her home in Ramallah.

CAIRO PAPERS IN SOCIAL SCIENCE

Volume Twelve 1989

1   *Cairo's Leap Forward: People, Households and Dwelling Space,* Fredric Shorter
2   *Women, Water and Sanitation: Household Water Use in Two Egyptian Villages,* Samiha el-Katsha et al.
3   Palestinian Labor in a Dependent Economy: Women Workers in the West Bank Clothing Industry, Randa Siniora
4   The Oil Question in Egyptian-Israeli Relations, 1967–1979: A Study in International Law and Resource Politics, Karim Wissa

Volume Thirteen 1990

1   *Squatter Markets in Cairo,* Helmi R. Tadros, Mohamed Feteeha, Allen Hibbard
2   *The Sub-culture of Hashish Users in Egypt: A Descriptive Analytic Study,* Nashaat Hassan Hussein
3   *Social Background and Bureaucratic Behavior in Egypt,* Earl L. Sullivan, el Sayed Yassin, Ali Leila, Monte Palmer
4   *Privatization: the Egyptian Debate,* Mostafa Kamel el-Sayyid

Volume Fourteen 1991

1   *Perspectives on the Gulf Crisis,* Dan Tschirgi and Bassam Tibi
2   *Experience and Expression: Life Among Bedouin Women in South Sinai,* Deborah Wickering
3   Impact of Temporary International Migration on Rural Egypt, Atef Hanna Nada
4   *Informal Sector in Egypt,* Nicholas S. Hopkins ed.

Volume Fifteen, 1992

1   *Scenes of Schooling: Inside a Girls' School in Cairo,* Linda Herrera
2   Urban Refugees: Ethiopians and Eritreans in Cairo, Dereck Cooper
3   Investors and Workers in the Western Desert of Egypt: An Exploratory Survey, Naeim Sherbiny, Donald Cole, Nadia Makary
4   *Environmental Challenges in Egypt and the World,* Nicholas S. Hopkins, ed.

Volume Sixteen, 1993

1   *The Socialist Labor Party: A Case Study of a Contemporary Egyptian Opposition Party,* Hanaa Fikry Singer
2   *The Empowerment of Women: Water and Sanitation Iniatives in Rural Egypt,* Samiha el Katsha, Susan Watts
3   The Economics and Politics of Structural Adjustment in Egypt: Third Annual Symposium
4   *Experiments in Community Development in a Zabbaleen Settlement,* Marie Assaad and Nadra Garas

Volume Seventeen, 1994

Volume Eighteen, 1995

Volume Nineteen, 1996

Volume Twenty, 1997

Volume Twenty-one, 1998

Volume Twenty-two, 1999

1   *Poverty and Poverty Alleviation Strategies in Egypt,* Ragui Assaad and Malak Rouchdy
2   *Between Field and Text: Emerging Voices in Egyptian Social Science,* Seteney Shami and Linda Hererra, eds.
3   *Masters of the Trade: Crafts and Craftspeople in Cairo, 1750–1850,* Pascale Ghazaleh
4   *Discourses in Contemporary Egypt: Politics and Social Issues,* Enid Hill, ed.

Volume Twenty-three, 2000

1   *Fiscal Policy Measures in Egypt: Public Debt and Food Subsidy,* Gouda Abdel-Khalek and Karima Korayem
2   *New Frontiers in the Social History of the Middle East,* Enid Hill, ed.
3   *Egyptian Encounters,* Jason Thompson, ed.
4   *Women's Perception of Environmental Change in Egypt,* Eman el Ramly

Volume Twenty-four, 2001

1, 2   *The New Arab Family,* Nicholas S. Hopkins, ed.
3   *An Investigation of the Phenomenon of Polygyny in Rural Egypt,* Laila S. Shahd
4   *The Terms of Empowerment: Islamic Women Activists in Egypt,* Sherine Hafez

Volume Twenty-five, 2002

1, 2   *Elections in the Middle East: What do they Mean?* Iman A. Hamdy, ed.
3   *Employment Crisis of Female Graduates in Egypt: An Ethnographic Account,* Ghada F. Barsoum
4   *Palestinian and Israeli Nationalism: Identity Politics and Education in Jerusalem,* Evan S. Weiss

Volume Twenty-six, 2003

1   *Culture and Natural Environment: Ancient and Modern Middle Eastern Texts,* Sharif S. Elmusa, ed.
2   *Street Children in Egypt: Group Dynamics and Subcultural Constituents,* Nashaat Hussein
3   *IMF–Egyptian Debt Negotiations,* Bessma Momani
4   *Forced Migrants and Host Societies in Egypt and Sudan,* Fabienne Le Houérou

Volume Twenty-seven, 2004

1&2   *Cultural Dynamics in Contemporary Egypt,* Maha Abdelrahman, Iman A. Hamdy, Malak Rouchdy and Reem Saad (eds.)
3   *The Role of Local Councils in Empowerment and Poverty Reduction,* Solava Ibrahim
4   *Beach Politics: Gender and Sexuality in Dahab,* Mutafa Abdalla

Volume Twenty-eight, 2005

Volume Twenty-nine, 2006

★ currently out of print

ملخص

يشتمل هذا العدد على أبحاث تناولت حالات إنسانية مختلفةً بين الفلسطينيين، تتراوح بين ساكني قرى قُسِمت بالحدود مثل "الخط الأخضر" (خط هدنة عام ١٩٤٩) وسكان من أصل فلسطيني قُطِعَت جذورهم في فلسطين ويريدون الآن أن يُؤسِّسوا حياتهم وحياة أطفالهم خارج فلسطين وحتى خارج العالم العربي. وتتعامل هذه الدراسات مع العوامل الاجتماعية والاقتصادية المؤثِّرة في العودة، والجهود الحقيقية والافتراضية للعودة إلى فلسطين من قبل مجموعتين مختلفتين جداً (مجموعة الشباب ومجموعة الخبراء المهنيين).

ان الموضوع الرئيسي الجامع لهذه المساهمات هو دور الحدود الجغرافية والحواجز- تلك التي يحاول الناسِ عبورها وتلك التي خلقتها الصيرورات السياسية حول السكان (مثل الخط الأخضر والجدار الإسرائيلي). يتنقل البعض ويهاجر، بينما يطوِّر آخرون استراتيجيات البقاء للتعامل مع واقع سياسي يعرقل حركتهم. وتعتبر حرية الحركة وعرقلتها جزءاً من المعرفة السوسيولوجية التي يشكل استشفافها ضرورة لفهم اختيارات اللاجئين بخصوص هجرة العودة. ونحن نستخدم كلمة "هجرة" هنا لنؤكد أن الحركة باتجاه فلسطين هي حالة هجرة لا حالة عودة إلى الوطن الأصلي. وتشكل أبحاث هذا الكتاب مساهمات لفهم المعضلات التي واجهت الشرائح المختلفة من السكان الفلسطينيين في الفترة التي سبقت بناء الحائط الإسرائيلي، بداية من عام ٢٠٠٥؛ الحائط الذي قطع أكثر أوصالهم وقسم المناطق الفلسطينية ومنع بعض أنماط الحركة التي ظهرت منذ اتفاقية أوسلو في العام ١٩٩٣ ("إعلان المبادئ").

يطرح ساري حنفي في الفصل الأول محاولة لفهم سوسيولوجي لعودة اللاجئين الفلسطينيين من خلال أبحاث ميدانية أجراها على مدى عقد من الزمن، بما في ذلك مسح قام به مركز "شمل" ويبحث بعض العوامل التي ستؤثِّر على قرار اللاجئين في حركتهم المستقبلية، وخاصة فيما يتعلق بالعودة والرأسمال الاجتماعي. بينما تحلل شيرين الأعرج (الفصل الثاني) دراسة حالة الروابط الاجتماعية لأهالي قرية الولجة بين القرية والمهجر. وقد حافظ أهالي الولجة، رغم التبعثر، على أشكال مختلفة من العلاقات، بما في ذلك العلاقات الذرائعية والمصلحية في أثناء انتخابات جمعية الولجة.

وتقدم ماري توتري (الفصل الثالث) وسيدريك باريزو (الفصل الرابع) دراستين مرتكزتين على أبحاث ميدانية داخل الخط الأخضر حول تغيير الحدود والحواجز، ومعه الواقع والهوية، من خلال دراسة حالة قرية برطعة المشطورة، والروابط القرابية لبدو النقب بين غزة والضفة الغربية والأردن. لقد بينا أن حركة التواصل عبر الحدود سعت للتكيف مع هذه الحدود بدلاً من تحديها، وأظهرا كيف تخلق الحدود علاقات القوة وتمهد الطريق لنشوء النزاعات.

يقوم محمد كامل درعي (الفصل الخامس) بدراسة مسارات اللاجئين الفلسطينيين في لبنان منذ بداية التسعينيات؛ هؤلاء الفلسطينيون الذين يحاولون إيجاد مكان أكثر أمنا من لبنان، فيتوجهون نحو أوروبا، ويستخدمون القرابة مصدراً من مصادر تسهيل الهجرة. وتدرس تمارا تميمي (الفصل السادس) تعاطي الشباب الفلسطيني- الأمريكي العائد مع إشكالية الهوية، وتظهر لنا ببراعة كيف تعامل هؤلاء الشباب مع ولاءاتهم المتعددة. وهي تقدم حالة مثيرة من مفاوضات الهوية بينهم و بين أعضاء عائلاتهم حول العيش في الضفة الغربية.

وأخيراً يُقيِّم ساري حنفي حجم "العودة" إلى الأراضي الفلسطينية منذ اتفاقيات أوسلو، ومساهمة الشتات في بناء الكيان الفلسطيني من دون عودته الفيزيائية وعن طريق المعرفة والخبرة. وقد ركز على تجربتين: الأولى هي برنامج نقل المعرفة عبر المغتربين يُدعى "توكتن" (Tokten) بهدف استقدام علماء وتكنولوجيين فلسطينيين إلى وطنهم الأم. والثانية تجربة أسستها السلطة الوطنية الفلسطينية على شكل شبكة إنترنتية لربط العلماء والخبراء المغتربين الفلسطينيين مع الداخل، والاستفادة من كفاءات العلماء للتنمية في فلسطين، وهي تسمى "باليستا" (Palesta).

بحـوث القـاهـرة
فى العلـوم الاجتماعيـة

مجلد ٢٩   عدد ١   ربيع ٢٠٠٦

عبور الحدود وتبدل الحواجز:
دراسات في الحالة الفلسطينية

تحرير
ساري حنفي

المشاركون
شيرين الأعرج
سيدريك باريزو
محمد كامل درعي
تمارا تميمي
ماري توتري

قسم النشر بالجامعة الامريكية بالقاهرة
القاهرة – نيويورك